Beyond the Bedtime Story

Other Titles by Nicholas D. Young

Betwixt and Between: Understanding and Meeting the Social and Emotional Development Needs of Students During the Middle School Transition Years (2014)

Educational Entrepreneurship: Promoting Public-Private Partnerships for the 21st Century (2015)

Transforming Special Education Practices: A Primer for School Administrators and Policy Makers (2012)

Beyond the Bedtime Story

Promoting Reading Development during the Middle School Years

Nicholas D. Young and Christine N. Michael

ROWMAN & LITTLEFIELD
Lanham • Boulder • New York • London

Published by Rowman & Littlefield
A wholly owned subsidiary of The Rowman & Littlefield Publishing Group, Inc.
4501 Forbes Boulevard, Suite 200, Lanham, Maryland 20706
www.rowman.com

Unit A, Whitacre Mews, 26-34 Stannary Street, London SE11 4AB

Copyright © 2015 by Nicholas D. Young and Christine N. Michael

British Library Cataloguing in Publication Information Available

Library of Congress Cataloging-in-Publication Data

Library of Congress Cataloging-in-Publication Data Available
ISBN 978-1-4758-1114-8 (cloth : alk. paper) -- ISBN 978-1-4758-1115-5 (pbk. : alk. paper) -- ISBN 978-1-4758-1116-2 (electronic)

♾ ™ The paper used in this publication meets the minimum requirements of American National Standard for Information Sciences Permanence of Paper for Printed Library Materials, ANSI/NISO Z39.48-1992.

Printed in the United States of America

Contents

Preface

Beyond the Bedtime Story: Promoting Reading Development during the Middle School Years was written for practitioners and educators, classroom teachers and school administrators, as well as parents and policymakers who are deeply invested in the reading development and academic success of middle school students. While this book largely focuses on understanding and addressing the difficulties that can accompany the reading process, it also is intended to be used as a platform to promote the myriad of benefits of reading. While much has been written about literacy and learning difficulties at the elementary level, few scholars and practitioners have focused their writings on these issues at the middle school level.

The motivation for writing this book comes from several concerns:

- *Our belief that young adolescents are in a unique developmental period— one that is distinctly different from late childhood or adolescence itself— and one that merits special attention;*
- *Our concern about the troubling numbers of middle school students who struggle with the act of reading, both in and out of school;*
- *Our knowledge that reading quality literature plays a powerful role in positive child development;*
- *Our awareness that middle school is when many students will disengage academically if they cannot read at grade level;*
- *Our years of experience in educating parents, teachers, school counselors, and other helping professionals that has led to the recognition that there is age-specific knowledge that could assist them in helping young adolescents become more proficient and involved readers;*
- *Our interest in identifying and sharing best practices that lead to middle school reading success.*

We chose the title *Beyond the Bedtime Story* on purpose, in recognition of the fact that middle school is that time at which the very purpose for reading appears to change. Instead of reading for literacy development and for pleasure, academic reading now takes on a content-driven focus.

Parents and caregivers may be less likely to continue cherished traditions of reading aloud with their children, despite the fact, as several of the book's contributors mention, early adolescents still rank "read alouds" as one of their favorite activities. Middle school students may be more reticent to ask for help, and those who care about them may feel less knowledgeable about how to support their literacy development at this age. Additionally, there may be confusion about what kinds of materials make for "valuable" reading experiences.

Young adolescence is a time of many transitions for the middle school students trying to navigate it. By recognizing the nature of this developmental period, educators, caregivers, and other helping professionals can promote pro-social development. Building students' sense of efficacy through improved reading skills and offering them opportunities to work through developmental issues and personal challenges by seeing how literary figures—true and fictional—have done it before them are things that all of us can do. Creating a strong cadre of fluent readers requires school, community, and home commitment.

The concerns noted above are the foci of the chapters of this book. We have attempted to balance theory, research, proven best practice, and the experiences of middle school students and their teachers as we depict the hurdles that young adolescent readers face and the approaches that may assist them. This book takes a multifaceted approach in that it highlights both the academic and socio-emotional components of reading.

Written by a highly seasoned team of practitioners and scholars, this text attempts to fill the void in texts on middle school reading by providing a foundational understanding of typical reading development, reading disorders, and effective interventions when reading challenges arise. Consistent with other practitioner-oriented sources, this book seeks to offer a truncated review of relevant literature followed by suggestions to guide practice.

It is our hope that all who play powerful roles in the education and development of young adolescents will glean useful strategies to promote and strengthen their reading skills, attitudes, and habits. By providing contact information for the chapter authors, we wish to encourage readers to reach out to them for further information or to engender discussions about what they have found to be successful in their middle school reading practice.

Acknowledgments

We are deeply appreciative of the time and professional expertise that each of the contributing authors lent to this book. All of them are accomplished scholars and practitioners who have made a lasting contribution to the field of education; thus, it was a true privilege for us to have had this opportunity to collaborate with each one of them.

We also wish to publicly thank Sue Clark of Holyoke, Massachusetts, for her careful review of the final draft of this book. She has become a truly invaluable member of our support team, and her contributions are both recognized and sincerely appreciated. On a personal note, we would like to recognize Ellen Noonan, Richard Holzman, and Paula Goodreau for their collective support of our own scholarly and professional endeavors. Their ongoing encouragement matters far more than they may realize.

And last, but not least, we want to acknowledge and thank teachers everywhere who strive each and every day to educate the next generation of students. As a career in teaching has become ever more demanding given the plethora of new state and federal mandates, those who are willing to take on this challenge have earned our complete admiration and respect.

—Nicholas D. Young and Christine N. Michael

Introduction

While contemporary educators may disagree about many things, their alarm regarding the growing numbers of students who cannot read proficiently is not one of them. The literacy rates among elementary students are troubling at best. Studentsfirst.org (2015) reports that according to the 2013 National Assessment of Education Progress reading test, 66 percent of current U.S. fourth graders were below proficient (not reading at grade level). Factor in socio-economic status, and the results are even more disturbing: among students from low-income backgrounds, 80 percent score below grade level in reading.

Sadly, evidence suggests middle school students fare poorly on reading proficiency measures as well. For example, the 2013 National Assessment of Education Progress reading test revealed that roughly 22 percent of eighth graders scored below the "basic" level, with only 36 percent of eighth graders at or above grade level (Studentsfirst, 2015). Depending on the author, 1 in 5 or 4 in 10 students will experience difficulties in reading (Hamilton & Glascoe, 2006; Kass & Maddux, 2005). Of these students, 75 percent who have reading disabilities and are not identified prior to third grade continue to have reading difficulties in ninth grade (Hamilton & Glascoe, 2006; National Center for Learning Disabilities, 2005).

Upon further examination, studies also show a growing literacy gap between boys and girls (Sadowski, 2010) and a higher percentage of boys with reading difficulties (Donahue, Finnegan, Lutkus, Allen, & Campbell, 2000; Snow, Burns, & Griffin, 1998). Perhaps most disturbing is that the majority of students with reading disabilities frequently fail to catch up to their same age peers and may suffer from a lifetime of low self-esteem (Connor, Alberto, Compton, & O'Connor, 2014; Clay, 1991).

Introduction

When heavy emphasis is placed on learning to read in the early grades, including using best teaching practices and research driven interventions used with fidelity and consistent assessment, many reading difficulties can be overcome. However, for those same students, it is vital to have literacy instruction in the upper grades that is coordinated, comprehensive, and focused on maintaining the positive gains made in the younger grades (Biancarosa & Snow, 2006). This two-pronged approach is the best defense for students at risk.

Research shows that the older the child and wider the learning gap, the more difficult it is to remediate due to the fact that the reading difficulties become "entrenched and intractable" (Coyne, Zipoli, & Ruby, 2006, p. 166). The National Center for Learning Disabilities (2005) states that while teaching older children to read is more difficult, 90 percent to 95 percent of these students can be successful when given the appropriate interventions. These students may never become expert readers, but at the least will be proficient and able to take control of their future without feeling like a failure.

There is a clear difference between learning to read and reading to learn. The former takes place in the early elementary years and refers to decoding, phonics, fluency, vocabulary, and comprehension (National Reading Panel, 2000). The latter, reading to learn, encompasses late elementary, the middle school years, and beyond, and requires students to read for the understanding and assimilation of information as well as academic enhancement. Available research reminds us that reading for content requires our students to be able to decode 95 percent of the words on a page and understand 90 percent of the vocabulary in the text, which are difficult hurdles to overcome (Allington & Johnston, 2002; Punkoney, 2013).

Given that we know that reading takes on even greater prominence in the high school years due to the increased emphasis placed on reading for content knowledge, as well as on literary analysis, it is essential that middle school students become proficient readers to avoid falling behind their same age peers. Recent national focus on initiatives addressing science, technology, engineering, and math, and the Common Core heighten the importance of promoting reading proficiency.

Despite numerous approaches and strategies, the 2012 Nation's Report Card shows that the average math and reading scores of American seventeen-year-olds has remained relatively stagnant since the 1970s (Institute of Education Services, 2012). According to the 2012 analysis conducted by the Programme for International Student Assessment, the United States ranks twenty-seventh out of thirty-four in math and twentieth in science (Organisation for Economic Co-operation and Development, 2012). With reading for understanding at the heart of all of these assessments and a global economy hungry for students skilled in these areas, we simply cannot afford to have middle schoolers entering the secondary level in need of remediation in reading.

A good deal has been written about reading at the elementary level; however, the topic of middle school literacy is underrepresented in scholarly literature. It is for this reason that this book attempts to address a series of critical questions: What role can reading play in early adolescent development? What specific challenges do middle school readers present in academic and family literacy settings? What works? Thus, the chapters are organized to move from an explication of the challenges to contemporary middle school literacy to interventions that have proven successful and finally to evidence-based practices and programs that can be utilized. The following brief overview gives readers a map for what can be found between the book's covers.

Chapter 1 was written by Nicholas D. Young and Christine N. Michael to provide a context for understanding the challenges associated with middle school reading development. Here, the authors point out the decline in reading for pleasure, how the testing culture has minimized the focus on literacy, and how overscheduling students has reduced the time available to address the myriad literacy needs that accompany the middle school transition. The authors discuss the nature of contemporary middle school students' struggles to see reading as engaging, necessary, and desirable when compared to the array of other activities available to them.

In chapter 2, Christine N. Michael provides a framework for understanding the developmental nature of reading in middle school with a unique emphasis on its relationship to finding a sense of self and place in the world. A hallmark of middle school is for students to develop a sense of personal identity and to find a peer group, both of which can have powerful links to literacy and language skills instruction in the classroom. While much of the shift in emphasis from elementary to middle school reading relates to greater emphasis on reading for content, the author argues that reading can play a powerful role in pro-social development among early adolescents and should be valued in that capacity as well.

Appreciating that reading comes with its own set of required skills in middle school, chapter 3, written by Sandra Donah, is aptly focused on what reading instruction should entail during these critical middle grades. The author stresses the need for direct reading instruction beyond the elementary years to focus on the complex literacy needs and weaknesses of struggling middle and high school readers. She covers essential topics in reading instruction at this level, including motivation, decoding, fluency, and vocabulary development.

With so much interest in the relationship between the brain and educational success in the field of education, this book would not have been complete without also examining this topic in depth. Written by Toni Spinelli-

Nannen and Roberta Green, chapter 4 offers a straightforward explanation of how the brain and reading development have a symbiotic relationship, providing further support for the importance of effective reading instruction. The authors break down complex scientific information into user-friendly material that family members and educators can employ to help students read more efficiently.

In chapter 5, Frank E. Vargo, Nicholas D. Young, and Richard D. Judah offer a practical review of what a reading disability is, as well as likely causes and effects. The authors point out, among other things, that a comprehensive approach to understanding and addressing reading disorders requires a thorough exploration of related factors, such as the possible presence of attention-deficit/hyperactivity disorder or attention difficulties, sensory deficits, emotional and behavioral disorders, and socio-environmental issues. Through this chapter readers will, then, gain a deeper understanding of common reading disabilities and disorders as well as how to approach interventions for addressing them.

Educators often acknowledge the importance of engaging families in comprehensive remediation plans. Chapter 6, written by Julie DeRoach, provides parents (and the educators who make recommendations to them) with practical suggestions on how to become directly involved. Although the transition to middle school marks a period of time in which families may disengage from the level of involvement they had with their children in elementary school, this is a critical time for family support. Through such approaches as charting progress, developing routines, employing technology, and using one or more of the home-based strategies presented, families can be more effective partners in helping struggling middle school readers.

In chapter 7, Timothy C. Allen and Christine N. Michael offer proven approaches that high-performing educators can use to engage reluctant readers. Several of the recommendations are supported by direct quotes from classroom teachers who have had a lasting and positive impact on their students. Critical considerations are underscored, including approaches for marketing the importance of reading to middle schoolers and the need to celebrate achievements. The writers involved with drafting this book consider these topics quite fitting for inclusion in the text, as they fully support the idea that middle school is an essential developmental period where education professionals need to use every option available to encourage preteens and early teens to make reading and academic achievement their top priorities.

Written by Nicholas D. Young and Elizabeth Jean, chapter 8 was included to provide a more complete picture of popular reading programs and teacher-generated approaches to reading instruction. With so many different reading programs currently on the market, education stakeholders should have a better understanding of which particular ones are considered research based. Classroom approaches that complement full reading programs are also offered to create a more complete picture of best practices in reading instruction at the middle school level.

Last but not least, the authors of chapter 9, Jennifer S. Alexander and Nicholas D. Young, provide an overview of the response to intervention framework and explain how it can be employed in a middle school setting to assist teachers and administrators with developing effective intervention strategies to aid unskilled readers. A series of evidence-based, individualized reading interventions that have been found to be effective when working with struggling readers are also presented as an easy-to-use reference guide. As parents and educators, the authors sought to end this book optimistically with a chapter that features the most promising options available to help all middle school students pursue reading proficiency.

REFERENCES

Allington, R. L., & Johnston, P. (2002). Reading to learn: Lessons from exemplary fourth grade classrooms. New York, NY: Guilford Press.

Biancarosa, C., & Snow, C. E. (2006). Reading next - A vision for action and research in middle and high school literacy: A report to Carnegie Croporation of New York (2nd ed.). Washington, DC: Alliance for Excellent Education.

Clay, M. M. (1991). Becoming literate: The construction of inner control. Portsmouth, NH: Heinemann.

Connor, C. M., Alberto, P. A., Compton, D. L., & O'Connor, R. E. (2014). Improving reading outcomes for students with or at risk for reading disabilities: A synthesis of the contributions from the Institute of Education Sciences Research Center (NCSER2014-3000). Washington, DC: National Center for Educational Research, Institute of Education Sciences, U.S. Department of Education.

Coyne, M. D., Zipoli, R. P., & Ruby, J. R. (2006). Beginning reading instruction for students at risk for learning disabilities: What, how, and when. Intervention in School and Clinic, 41, 161–68.

Donahue, P. L., Finnegan, R. J., Lutkus, A. D., Allen, N. L., & Campbell, J. R. (2000). The nation's report card: Fourth-grade reading. Retrieved from http://nces.ed.gov/pubsearch/pubsinfo.asp?

Hamilton, S., & Glascoe, F. P. (2006). Evaluation of children with reading difficulties. American Family Physician, 74(12), 2079–86.

Kass, C. E., & Maddux, C. D. (2005). A human development view of learning disabilities: From theory to practice. Springfield, IL: Charles C. Thomas Publisher, Ltd.

National Center for Learning Disabilities (2005). Annual report. New York: NY. Retrieved from http://www.ncld.org/up-content/uploads/2014/12/2005/annualreport .pdf.

National Reading Panel. (2000). Teaching children to read: An evidence based assessment of the scientific research literature on reading and its implications for reading instruction. Reports of the subgroups. Washington, DC: National Institute of Child Health and Human Development.

National Center for Education Statistics. (2012). NAEP 2012: Trends in academic progress. (NCES 2013-456). Washington, DC: U.S. Department of Education. Retrieved from http://nces.ed.gov/nationsreportcard/subject/publications/main2012/pdf/2013456.pdf.

Organisation for Economic Co-operation and Development. (2012). Country note: Programme for international student assessment: Results from PISA 2012. Retrieved from http://www.oecd.org/unitedstates/PISA-2012-results-US.pdf.

Punkoney, S. (2013). How children learn to read: What the research tells us about decoding and the brain. Retrieved from http://stayathomneeducator.com/how-children-learn-to-read-what-the-research-tells-us-about-decoding-and-the-brain.

Sadowski, M. (2010). Putting the boys in crisis in context. Education Digest, 76(3), 10–13.

Snow, C. E., Burns, M. S., & Griffin, P. (Eds.). (1998). Preventing reading difficulties in young children. Washington, DC: National Academies Press.

Studentsfirst.org, (2015). Statistics about education in America. Retrieved from https://www.studentsfirst.org/pages/the-stats.

Chapter One

Setting the Context for Understanding the Challenges to Middle School Literacy

Nicholas D. Young and Christine N. Michael

"What went wrong?" Kjersti VanSlyke-Briggs (2011) asks in the title of her two-year study on the increase in "aliteracy" among middle grade students. By using the term *aliteracy*, she references those students who are capable enough readers but who choose not to read. Although some of these aliterate students eventually will return to an interest in reading for pleasure later in their lives, VanSlyke-Briggs (2011) notes that others never regain the love of reading that they possessed in elementary grades, and still more struggle with reading their content assignments in class.

Considerable scholarly work on the decline of reading among middle school students has focused on ways to keep students interested. There is, however, a dearth of research on the actual causes of reading problems in the middle grades. Even fewer studies ask students themselves to identify the causes.

What is not debated in any of these articles is the reality that reading among adolescents is declining. According to Bradshaw (2004) in a National Endowment of the Arts report, they are reading less and for shorter amounts of time. In addition, the report claims that even when they read, they are apt to be simultaneously engaged in other media activities. The 2004 study echoed findings similar to one written by Ball (2004), also for the National Endowment of the Arts, although that study considered only traditional literacies.

Reading for pleasure, within both school and family settings, is considered a birthright of early childhood. Parents and other family members see encouraging and participating in literacy activities with children as a primary

1

role. Communities typically offer library story hours and celebrate the achievements of literary giants, such as Dr. Seuss, in annual events. Schools frequently tell students to "Drop Everything and Read." Nevertheless, as children turn into early adolescents, reading competently—and for pleasure—becomes more challenging.

Katy, a student interviewee in Beers' (2005) study on middle school reading, captures the shift in the very definition of reading as a student transitions from the elementary classroom. She admits that she enjoys reading magazines, but Katy does not believe that her teacher would consider reading a magazine "reading." "It is reading for you to learn about comprehension things. You study like predict and fact and opinion. You can tell that it is [reading] because of the, like, questions you always get asked" (Beers, 2005, p. 7). Katy confesses, "I've never thought about a book being something that I might think about, you know, emotionally. The teachers always told me what to think. . . . Reading seems pretty boring, pretty useless. I just don't feel any motivation to do it" (Beers, 2005, p. 7).

THE LEGACY OF ELEMENTARY SCHOOL

Notably, every single participant in VanSlyke-Briggs' (2011) qualitative study "noted that they enjoyed reading as a child. Many of the students shared that they had participated in motivating school programs, but that they liked to read outside of the programs as well. . . . Personal literacy histories included a nighttime story, trips to the public library, books read by parents and older siblings as modeling literate behaviors, and freedom of choice in reading selections" (VanSlyke-Briggs, 2011, p. 6).

The researcher found three key elements in the positive view of elementary reading: free time to read, choice of reading materials, and the perception of reading as a social event—a perception encouraged in school, the family, and the community. Students also recalled enjoying larger-scale literacy initiatives, including book clubs, ordering from the Scholastic book orders, contests sponsored at the school level, and efforts promoted by Pizza Hut and other vendors.

THE ROLE OF FAMILY

In Beers' (2005) study, middle school readers recalled many reading activities within their families, dating back to as early as they could remember. When their parents were interviewed, they confirmed the following practices: they read frequently to their children; they read for long periods of time; they read during different times of the day and in different places; they kept books and other reading materials in their homes and cars; and if they placed their children in child care settings, they made certain that literacy held primacy in the curriculum (Beers, 2005). These children enter school in what Early (1960) calls "unconscious delight," holding an "aesthetic" stance towards books and reading.

However, a 2014 Scholastic study found that of the one thousand children surveyed, 40 percent (or four in ten) "say they wished their parents had continued reading aloud to them" (Scholastic & YouGov, 2014, p. 6). Children who have not been read to and who have not grown up seeing reading modeled as an important and pleasurable activity enter schools with a shorter time in which to enter that "delight." The older they get, the more they read for content, comprehension, and assessment of what they know. If children in non-reading families were read to, it was at bedtime and was viewed, as one participant confided, as "an activity meant to keep me quiet and make me go to sleep" (Beers, 2005, p. 16).

THE TRANSITION TO MIDDLE SCHOOL

A salient component of the reading challenge may lie in the actual transition to middle school itself. As VanSlyke-Briggs (2011) points out, the transition from elementary to middle school has always been a difficult one, and in many schools, this development now happens both actually and symbolically at a much younger grade level. The "whole child" attitude of elementary school culture changes significantly, and the expectations for academic rigor increase dramatically. For many students, middle school simply is overwhelming. One of VanSlyke-Briggs' (2011) participants recalled:

> In middle school, I didn't read at all, only what I had to for class. It was a crazy time; middle school is always crazy. I had a lot of different classes, and I don't think I read at all on my own. I wasn't really encouraged, I mean not that they didn't encourage it, but it wasn't really anything set up or like read on your own, it was like flopping around class to class, and most kids didn't read much. (p. 9)

In addition to figuring out the more complex schedule and variety of classes, middle school students are faced with a daunting array of physical, social, emotional, and cognitive changes. Among these milestones are ending one's childhood, separating from the internalized parents, finding a peer group, developing a unique identity, discovering one's racial and ethnic identity, exploring sexual identity, developing a sense of morality, acquiring self-esteem and self-actualization, and building personal assets.

THE CULTURE OF TESTING

There is growing concern that the effects of high-stakes testing are eroding the fundamental tenets of the middle school model. As represented in documents produced by such organizations as the National Middle School Association (2015), quality middle school education essentially is a continuation of the "whole child" approach to learning, with such practices as teaming, cooperative learning, flexible grouping, and social interaction at the heart of the classroom. Musoleno and White (2010) also point to the need to promote creative thinking and emotional development, including allowing young adolescents to learn about themselves.

All these components are integrated into a strong literacy program. However, as Butti (2008) notes, not only is there greater emphasis on testing and not on making personal, creative connections with what middle school students are reading, there are "fewer opportunities for students to read and respond to imaginative writing in general" (p. 3) in the contemporary middle school classroom.

Musoleno and White's (2010) study revealed that middle school teachers indeed felt that they have had to alter their pedagogy from best middle school practices to more test preparation, testing, pull-out for extra instruction, and fewer enrichment experiences; this is particularly true in math and language arts. "Attention to the learner is being replaced by attention to the test" (Musoleno & White, 2010, p. 8). As one teacher lamented, "increased testing and test preparation means that we have less time to actually teach engaging and interesting material that would leave a lasting memory on the student" (Musoleno & White, 2010, p. 8). This was the dominant sentiment of the study participants.

Lesesne (2006) reports that the joy of reading is being lost at even earlier ages than ever before, citing the drop that usually occurred around eighth grade now is often seen as early as fourth or fifth. As one of VanSlyke-Briggs' (2011) study participants told her, "In [eighth] grade, every two weeks there was a test and an essay on the book. It was just too much. I probably read two or three out of the assigned reading books. I didn't read for pleasure at all. I read the bare minimum—less than the minimum" (p. 10).

THE OVERSCHEDULED CHILD

Many of VanSlyke-Briggs' (2011) and Jacobsen's (2014) interviewees remarked that middle school presented numerous activities that competed directly with free time to read for pleasure. Most notably, sports, drama, arts, church, and community activities comprised a tantalizing array of activities that tapped their interests and allowed them to socialize with friends while engaging in the activities themselves.

As Jack candidly stated, "I didn't want to read from that point on, and then in middle school that's, like, when we all started to play sports, so I would rather play soccer or basketball than sit down and read a book. . . . There's too much other stuff you could be doing" (VanSlyke-Briggs, 2011, p. 8). Years ago, David Elkins (2003) sounded the alarm about the "over-scheduled child" and "hurried childhood," commenting that far too many children are "overbooked," leaving them little to no time for activities that can develop creativity, individuality, and the life of the mind.

Elkins (2003) stated "Children need time to read, write, think, dream, draw, build, create, fantasize, and explore social interests"; these very activities help students "clarify who they are and what they are truly interested in" (p. 3). Elkins (2003) also urges families to put activities in balance and make certain that students have "time to relax, talk, read, play games, and just hang out" with one another (p. 2). The aforementioned activities all play vital developmental roles in middle school students' lives.

MEETING MYRIAD LITERACY NEEDS

The learner populations in middle schools across this country are becoming increasingly diverse, making it even more challenging to create meaningful reading experiences. According to Garcia (2013), the foreign-born share of the U.S. population has more than doubled since the 1960s. The past decade saw a sizeable increase in the foreign-born population; between 2000 and 2011, there was a 30 percent increase, from 31.1 million to 40.04 million (Garcia, 2013).

The countries of origins of new immigrants are more diverse than they have been in the past. Many children now live in single-parent households, more than 20 percent of America's children live in poverty, and homelessness is rising (U.S. Census Bureau, 2011). The Office of Special Education Programs (1999) reports that over the past twenty years, the number of students with disabilities has grown at a faster pace than both the general population and school enrollment; according to this same source, approximately one in six children, with the vast majority in elementary and middle schools, falls into this category.

In terms of reading diversity, Beers (2005) identified patterns of responses among her interviewees when they were asked why they chose not to read. These patterns were organized into a typology that included five types of middle school readers: avid, dormant, uncommitted, unmotivated, and unskilled.

The avid reader identifies as a reader, makes time to read, sees reading as "a way of life," and has positive feelings about other readers. The second type, the dormant reader, shares most of these traits but does not make the time (or perhaps is not afforded the time in his or her busy schedule) to read. An "uncommitted" middle school reader may view other readers positively but sees reading's purpose as functional and pragmatic. Reading to this student is "knowing words."

The "unmotivated" reader neither enjoys reading nor views other readers in a positive light. Reading is a process of "saying words," but the words do not move the reader in any way other than imparting some functional knowledge. Finally, the "unskilled" reader is actually the illiterate middle schooler, perhaps with a kinder, gentler title. Such a student struggles to figure words out and has difficulty making sense of the text. He or she may not have negative feelings about reading, but such a student clearly cannot keep pace with what is expected of a reader in the middle school grades.

THE CHALLENGE

Holbrook (1983) plainly and insightfully summarizes the middle school reading challenge: "Young people who cannot read at all are far outnumbered by young people who can read (poorly or well) but won't. The latter, which choose not to read, for whatever reason, have little advantage over those who are illiterate" (p. 38). Beers' (2005) typology, which was outlined in the previous section, reveals how difficult it is to meet the needs of all students within any given middle school.

While one might think that avid readers are to be envied, they need academic challenges to keep them engaged, and they also may receive socially disparaging remarks from peers who see them as "nerds" or "geeks." Dormant readers may require help in finding quality time to integrate reading into their busy social and academic schedule, or they may be facing life challenges at home that dissipate time and energy from reading for pleasure.

Uncommitted and unmotivated readers need to see additional purposes for their reading and be introduced to various kinds of reading materials that will entice them into the process. Meanwhile, unskilled readers need both academic intervention and empathic support to be treated with dignity while upgrading their skills. In the final analysis, it is imperative to develop individualized approaches to meet the unique developmental reading needs of all middle school students. To achieve this, parents and educators must work collaboratively to set content and support literacy in order to ensure life-long learning success.

POINTS TO REMEMBER

- Families who model literate behaviors such as trips to the library, reading at bedtime, and reading to a young child by a sibling or parent lead to positive feelings about reading and better reading skills in middle school students.
- Positive feelings about reading are influenced by three key elements: (1) free time to read, (2) choice of reading materials, and (3) perception of reading as a social event.
- Overscheduling the child leads to reduced time for reading and a perceived notion that reading is not an important skill.
- There is little difference between the student who is a poor reader and the student who cannot read; however, the differences in how to teach these children varies greatly and provides a considerable challenge to educators.

REFERENCES

Ball, D. (2004). To read or not to read: A question of national consequence. National Endowment of the Arts. Retrieved from http://arts.gov/sites/default/files/ToRead.pdf.

Beers, K. (2005). Choosing not to read: Understanding why some middle schoolers just say no. Retrieved from http://www.csun.edu/~krowlands/Content/Academic_Resources/Reading/Useful%20Articles/Beers-Choosing%20not%20to%20Read.pdf.

Bradshaw, T. (2004). Reading at risk: A survey of literacy in America. National Endowment of the Arts. Retrieved from http://arts.gov/sites/default/files/ReadingAtRisk.pdf.

Butti, L. (2008, Summer). Whither creativity? Middle school VP report. NYSEC News. Albany, NY: New York State English Council.

Early, M. (1960). Stages of growth in literacy appreciation. English Journal, 49 (3), 161–67.

Elkins, D. (2003, January 1). The overbooked child. Psychology Today. Retrieved from https://www.psychologytoday.com/articles/200301/the-overbooked-child.

Garcia, A. (2013). The facts on immigration today. Washington, DC: Center for American Progress. Retrieved from https://www.americanprogress.org/issues/immigration/report/2014/10/23/59040/the-facts-on-immigration-today-3/.

Holbrook, H. (1983). Motivating reluctant readers: A gentle push. In J. Thomas & R. Loring (Eds.), Motivating children and young adults to read (pp. 29–31). Phoenix, AZ: Oryx Press.

Jacobsen, L. (2014). Why boys don't read. Retrieved from http://www.greatschools.org/students/academic-skills/6832-why-so-many-boys-do-not-read.gs.

Lesesne, T. (2006). Naked reading: Uncovering what tweens need to be lifelong readers. Portland, ME: Stenhouse.

Mach, A. (2011, December 13). Homeless children at a record high in US. Can the trend be reversed? Christian Science Montior. Retrieved from http://www.csmonitor.com/USA/Society/2011/1213/Homeless-children-at-record-high-in-US.-Can-the-trend-be-reversed.

Musoleno, R. R., & White, G. P. (2010). Influences of high-stakes testing on middle school mission and practice. Research on Middle Level Education, 34 (3), 1–10.

National Middle School Association. (2015). Retrieved from http://www.amle.org/BrowsebyTopic/LanguageArtsandLiteracy/tabid/103/Default.aspx.

Office of Special Education Programs. (1999). To assure the free appropriate public education of all children with disabilities: Twenty-first annual report to Congress on the implementation of the Individuals with Disabilities Education Act. Washington, DC: Office of Special Education Programs, U.S. Department of Education. Retrieved from http://www.ed.gov/offices/OSERS/OSEP/OSEP99AnlRpt.

Scholastic & YouGov. (2014). Kids & family reading report. 5th ed. Retrieved from http://www.scholastic.com/readingreport/Scholastic-KidsAndFamilyReadingReport-5thEdition.pdf?v=100.

U.S. Census Bureau. (2011). Retrieved from http://www.census.gov/acs/www/data_documentation/2011_release/.

VanSlyke-Briggs, K. (2011, Fall). What went wrong: Middle school students and aliteracy. North Carolina Middle School Association Journal, 26 (1), 1–12.

Chapter Two

Seeing the Self in Text

Developmental Implications of Reading for Middle School Students

Christine N. Michael

Most articles and books concerning the importance of the mastery of reading skills in middle school focus on the necessity of reading for academic content, as students begin the transition from general elementary literacy to a greater emphasis on subject matter. Far less has been written about the value of literature's role in helping adolescents develop their sense of unique self and place in the world.

While therapists have long been known to use "bibliotherapy" as a healing tool, everyday reading of quality literature at the crucial early adolescent stage can provide its own kind of developmental therapy for middle school students. In addition, allowing a wider range of reading materials into the academic curriculum can help lure reluctant readers into the act of engaging with the text.

WHAT ARE THE DEVELOPMENTAL TASKS OF EARLY CHILDHOOD?

As will be outlined in this chapter, there are a number of important tasks of early adolescence, and each holds a kind of developmental primacy during the middle school years.

Early Adolescence Is Essentially the End of Childhood

Kroger (2007) describes the transition to early adolescence as closing the book on "childhood proper" (p. 5). Within this transition are the challenges of bringing into question what Kroger (2007) calls "the sameness and continuity" that marked the earlier years (p. 7). This is a period in which, as Erikson (1963) suggests, moratorium is necessary to attempt to integrate the self of early childhood and latency with the "demand for an enlarged sense of identity to encompass the physiological changes of puberty," as Kroger (2007, p. 38) describes it. Kroger (2007) also notes Kegan's (1982) concern that Erikson (1963) omitted a critical stage specific to early adolescence:

> I believe Erikson misses a stage between "industry" and "identity." His identity stage—with its orientation to the self alone, "Who am I?" time, achievement, ideology, self-certainty, and so on—captures some of late adolescence or early adulthood, but it does not really address the period of connection, inclusion, and highly invested mutuality which comes between the more independence-oriented periods of latency and late adolescent identity formation. (pp. 38–39)

Kegan (1982) proposed an additional stage—affiliation versus abandonment—as the major task of middle school. For many, identity formation is comprised of concerns with being liked, fitting in, and feeling accepted by desirable groups. As represented in statements by middle school students studied in both the United States and New Zealand (Kroger, 2007), being accepted or left out by peers is a prevalent identity concern for this age group, in addition to being recognized and supported by family.

Separating from the Internalized Parents

Marcia (1980) also saw that early adolescence was a time to begin to free oneself from "the internalized parents." The internalized parent is represented in the early adolescent by standards, values, morals, or beliefs that the child has come to accept, essentially without scrutiny. Both aspirations and prohibitions are woven into the fabric of the early adolescent, but these may not represent the young person's true interests, desires, or personality.

It is clearly essential work of the middle school period to bring into question one's developmental legacy to begin growing into one's authentic self. Kroger (2007) notes "the early adolescent task of beginning to disengage from the internalized parents and starting to seek extra-familial outlets for emotional and sexual energy, until now bound up within the family triangle" (p. 40).

Finding a Peer Group

Maslow (1968) contended that a sense of belonging was a fundamental human need if self-esteem and self-actualization were to be accomplished. For young adolescents, attaining a sense of belonging lies in beginning the separation from family of origin and the internalized parents, and a move to seeking a peer group. This complements Brown and Knowles' (2007) belief that middle school is usually the first opportunity for young adolescents to make real choices; such choices most often involve social connections—being accepted by those one admires or aspires to be like:

> A new world opens up in middle school. This expanding social landscape creates questions in young adolescents' minds about how to get peers to like them. They begin to see that some kids are popular while others aren't. They wonder how that happens and how they can become part of the popular group. They question where they stand and wonder what their peers think of them. (p. 42)

Reviewing more than thirty years of research about early adolescents' friendships, Brown and Klute (2004) found that middle schoolers were likely to choose friends who shared similar interests; same gender, race, and ethnicity also characterized their friendships. The traits of equality and reciprocity were important in forming friendships, and the authors noted that girls displayed more intimacy in their friendships. This last finding, however, has been questioned by others (see Pollack, 1998, for example), who argue that boys simply demonstrate intimacy in ways that are different from girls.

The review of research also shows that there is a general movement away from the small-group interactions of childhood to larger groups in middle school. These groups may include cliques, which usually are gender specific and headed up by a powerful leader, and crowds, which are clusters of cliques and usually identified on the basis of geography, interests, abilities, ethnicity, socioeconomic status, or peer status (Brown & Klute, 2004). What is sadly clear is that those who struggle to build relationships in childhood continue to do so in early adolescence, and such individuals may become targets for social exclusion and even bullying.

Developing a Unique Identity

Marcia's (1980) seminal work on identity formation focused specifically on adolescents' identity development, beginning with early adolescence. Employing two criteria, exploration and commitment, Marcia (1980) proposed a model for categorizing adolescents in relation to their ego-identity status. *Exploration*, as one might imagine, describes the active engagement in thinking about and weighing the "goodness of fit" among all possible identities.

Commitment refers to either the presence or the absence of the early adolescent's individual ideology, role, or occupation.

Early adolescents might be categorized in one of four different identity statuses: identity diffusion, identity foreclosure, moratorium, and achievement. Those in diffusion are either not exploring or not committing, while those in foreclosure have "locked in" to a decision without exploration, usually because of pressures from family or society to come to an early plan. Students in the moratorium stage are exploring without committing and can benefit from being provided with many opportunities to develop skills and interests before they make a choice. Students in the achievement stage have come to an initial choice after they have been involved in meaningful exploration.

Discovering Racial and Ethnic Identity

According to Holcomb-McCoy (2014), ethnicity can play a powerful role in the identity development of minority youth. The author argues that middle school is the stage at which this identity development becomes most salient. She cites Phinney's (1989) three-stage model of ethnic identity in which the first stage is characterized by lack of active exploration of one's ethnic identity due to disinterest, lack of exposure, or unexamined ethnic attitudes handed down to the adolescent. This stage is similar to Marcia's (1980) notion of foreclosure.

An adolescent also may be in the process of exploring his or her ethnic identity without commitment; this is particularly prevalent when there are perceived differences between the youth's ethnic identity and the dominant culture. Exploration at this stage, usually involving learning more about one's culture, is similar to Marcia's (1980) moratorium. Ethnic identity is achieved when the adolescent makes a firm commitment to an initial ethnic identity.

Cross (1991), as cited in Brown and Knowles (2007), established a similar, but five-stage, theory of Black racial identity that includes pre-encounter, encounter, immersion, internalization, and internalization/commitment as similar steps in consolidating racial identity. As Gay (1994) points out, the concept of forming a sense of identity is more difficult for minority students, as they have developmental work to do individually and culturally.

Exploring Sexual Identity

Kroger (2007) notes that "early adolescence is a time of coming to terms with a new sense of sexual identity, which the biological changes of puberty bring" (p. 49). The sexual self of the adolescent is differentiated in three ways: sexual or gender identity, sex or gender role, and sexual orientation.

One's identity equates to one's feelings of being male, female, androgynous, or undifferentiated, while one's role relates to the way an individual expresses his or her biological gender in social settings, according to those settings' norms and stereotypes about appropriate behavior. In addition, the adolescent becomes aware of the objects of one's sexual interest. If those objects are at odds with societal norms, the middle schooler may repress or struggle with how to integrate internal truth with external pressures.

Acquiring Self-Esteem and Self-Actualization

Developing self-esteem is another task of this maturation period. In Rice and Dolgin's (2005) research, there are six perceptions that the preadolescent is continuously pondering about the self that influence his or her self-esteem: who I really am, who I think I am, who others think I am, who I think others think I am, who I think I will become, and who I think others want me to become.

According to Brown and Knowles (2007), the amount of self-esteem that middle school students have depends on four variables: the amount of perceived control over their circumstances, whether they are accepted by those from whom they desire acceptance, the need to be competent in what they undertake, and a sense of being virtuous to others. While *self-actualization* may seem too lofty a term to describe middle school aspirations and achievement, there is no question that identity formation is in full swing at this time, and adolescents are in a continuous quest to find aspects of personality that have "goodness of fit" for them.

Brown and Knowles (2007) explain this phase in terms of Erikson's (1963) identity versus role confusion stage: "Despite interest in conforming and belonging to a social group, young adolescents still want individuality. The need for confirmation by a social group is really a need for personal validation. Learning to be part of a social group is an important part of the successful transition to independence. More vital, perhaps, are attempts to understand 'self'" (Brown & Knowles, 2007, p. 53).

Building Assets

Assets and resiliency building can construct internal protectors in middle school students. Benard (1993) and Henderson and Milstein (1996) urge schools to institute activities and curriculum that can help adolescents build their assets through service to others and opportunities for leadership development. Brooks and Goldstein (2004) also believe that individuals can be helped to become more resilient. Characteristics of individuals with a "resilient mindset" include a feeling of self-control, empathy, compassion, realistic goal setting, good problem solving and communications skills, and sensing one's unique special nature while helping others to do the same (Brooks & Goldstein, 2004).

Developing a Sense of Morality

Moral development is a complex task for the early adolescent. Most, if not all, of his or her current moral and ethical beliefs have been inherited from family, community, culture, and faith tradition; yet, the values, attitudes, and character virtues that he or she develops in middle school are likely to be carried well beyond adolescence. How does a middle school student find a moral compass in the contemporary world, especially when the "black-and-white" moral decision making of childhood falls away?

Many researchers feel that middle school students inherently desire to help improve the world and are passionately committed to causes such as social justice, animal rights, and environmental concerns (Brown & Knowles, 2007; Caissy, 1994; Rice & Dolgin, 2005). However, "deciding what is 'right' is often a cloudy process for young adolescents, depending on the situations that arise in their lives and from whom they seek approval" (Brown & Knowles, 2007, p. 49).

Brighton (2007) stresses the additional impact of "conventional morality" (in the form of media, music, and other elements of popular culture) on sound moral reasoning. As cited in Brown and Knowles (2007), Wormelli (2003) goes so far as to say, "We middle school teachers need to provide even more experiences involving moral and abstract reasoning, planning, awareness of consequences, and the effects of one's words and actions on others" (p. 80–81).

Reading's Role in Early Adolescent Development

In multiple ways, reading can assist adolescents in positive personal development during their middle school years. Glazer (1991), as cited in Norton and Norton (2011), identifies four major ways that quality literature supports the emotional growth of children:

> First, literature shows children that many of their feelings are common to other children and that those feelings are normal and natural. Second, literature explores a feeling from several viewpoints, giving a fuller picture and providing a basis for naming the feeling. Third, actions of various characters show options for dealing with particular emotions. Fourth, literature makes clear that one person can experience many emotions and that these emotions sometimes conflict. (p. 20)

Norton and Norton (2011) further stress the role of reading in early adolescent development. As they point out, adolescents tend to be emotionally volatile and experience many anxieties. Boys at this stage may feel particular pressure to hide their emotions to "be cool" and "fit in," and the vast majority of middle school students feel bouts of self-consciousness and awkwardness (Norton & Norton, 2011, p. 22).

Identifying Personal Strengths

Brighton (2007) cites the Search Institute's list of the forty most important developmental assets that an adolescent can possess; as one might imagine, the more of these a young person has, the greater his or her possibility of flourishing. Among the internal assets, "reading for pleasure" is ranked twenty-fifth (Brighton, 2007, p. 149). Not only does reading provide a healthy activity for adolescents, but it serves as a means for assisting them in seeing other personal assets by identifying with books' characters. Some of the "positive identity assets" that the Search Institute ranks highly, according to Brighton (2007), are self-esteem, personal power, sense of purpose, and positive view of one's future.

Solving Problems

Books from all genres can be used in several types of problem solving with adolescents. In one application, educators may opt to use a particular book to intentionally teach problem-solving skills, while stocking the classroom with books and suggesting titles that individual students might like is another approach. Norton and Norton (2011) believe that books featuring problem-solving characters increase students' motivation to read:

> Problem-resolution books encourage readers to see themselves as successful problem solvers. In this response, readers relate to characters that are able to solve or resolve problems and vicariously associate with successful characters. This internal motivation of prestige enables a child to "vicariously become a person of significance, who receives attention and exerts influence and control." (p. 36–37)

A middle school teacher who intimately knows his or her students can make wise suggestions to build the esteem and problem-solving abilities of reluctant readers. Choosing such books for all-class reading and discussion also can boost the social skills of middle school readers. Seeing that different individuals may generate myriad possible solutions to the same problem gives students practice in considering alternative viewpoints and respecting the ideas of others.

Forming Pro-Social Attitudes

As noted earlier, adolescents have a strong sense of social justice and are resistant to what they view as imperfections and failures in the adult world, but they may often feel powerless to effect change or have unrealistic ideas about how to go about effecting such change. The skilled middle school teacher can use reading, either whole-class, individual, or small-group, to present and encourage discussion about fiction or nonfiction in which people overcome social injustice, improve the quality of life around them, or stand up and question things that they believe are wrong.

The use of biographies, historical fiction, and nonfiction can be incredibly valuable in this particular area of development:

> Many children who read well-written biographies feel as if the biographical subjects become personal friends. . . . There are brave men and women who conquer seas, encounter new continents, and explore space. There are equally brave and intelligent women and men who fight discrimination, change lives through their ministering or interventions, and overcome disabilities in their efforts to achieve. (Norton & Norton, 2011, p. 450)

Informational texts also can engender advocacy among adolescents. For example, Steven Swineburn's *Once a Wolf: How Wildlife Biologists Fought to Bring Back the Grey Wolf* or Jane Goodall's *The Chimpanzee Family Book* may appeal to tweens who are animal lovers, while Yann Arthus-Bertrand's *Our Living Earth: A Story of People, Ecology and Preservation* uses text and amazing photographs shot over thirty years to emphasize the need for environmental activism.

Works of fiction encourage middle school readers to contemplate how they would respond in situations faced by characters who are physically or cognitively different and facing teasing, exclusion, or bullying by peers. Similarly, there are now a host of excellent books available that tackle attitudes towards the elderly, the homeless, and those of different racial, religious, or ethnic backgrounds.

Norton and Norton's (2011) *Through the Eyes of a Child* and Norton's (2013) *Multicultural Children's Literature* contain excellent suggestions for additional reading selections. In brave characters who champion the rights of others, adolescents can find role models who demonstrate ways of being in the world while "doing the right thing." Interestingly, contemporary children's literature does not always conclude with a "happy ending," so young readers also are confronted with the realities of choosing poorly or choosing not to act at all.

Dealing with Life Crises

Counselors and educators can make use of reading activities in both formal and informal ways to help middle school students deal with life transitions and crises. In the more formal sense, counselors may employ bibliotherapy as the intervention of choice as students grapple with issues such as separation, loss, illness, or grief. Contemporary realistic fiction covers an array of topics once considered taboo, such as homelessness, death, divorce, sexual abuse, and violence. In the hands of skillful trained counselors, characters who go through these situations can offer reassurance to students that they possess the inner and outer resources to successfully navigate life's rough times.

Regarding realistic fiction, writer Beverly Cleary comments, "I'm more interested in writing about people than problems. *Dear Mr. Henshaw* is about a boy that had a problem, not a problem that had a boy" (Norton & Norton, 2011, p. 363). Cleary's point is that quality literature about controversial issues presents characters who offer hope to real individuals by modeling resiliency in the face of adversity.

Emily, an eighth grader, says, "I am most like Tris from *Divergent*. This is because she believes it is best to be brave. Also, she would do anything for her family and friends." Another middle school girl identifies with a character in *Labor Day*: "There's a boy my age who is a lot like me. He's like me because he's determined about everything and keeps his head held high no matter what problem he runs in to." Clearly, these young readers can perceive strengths in the books' characters that they also can see in themselves, thus deriving a sense of personal pride in how they model the positive attributes of literary figures.

Holcomb-McCoy (2014) warns counselors to consider the importance of ethnicity in middle school identity development, discovering that "school counselors should examine counseling strategies and resources they use for possible modification. For instance, implementing bibliotherapy with books that include all white characters reinforces lack of ethnic exploration and acceptance" (p. 6).

Engendering Difficult Conversations

The relatively new category of realistic fiction has stirred controversies in many schools and communities. Some critics believe that such fiction raises subjects that are "too hot to handle" in the classroom; others, however, believe that these works allow for significant discussion and personal development because of their highly engaging topics. Norton and Norton (2011) encourage teachers to tackle sensitive topics for three primary reasons:

(1) books about relevant sociological or psychological problems can give young people opportunities to grow in their thinking processes and to extend their experiences; (2) problems addressed in books can provide some children with opportunities for identification and allow other children opportunities to empathize with their peers; and (3) problems in books invite decisions, elicit opinions, and afford opportunities to take positions on issues. (p. 367)

Having a wide variety of books in the classroom for free reading and choosing those texts that convey real-life situations middle school students might encounter can assist young readers in better understanding dilemmas they potentially may face. Discussion is a large part of meaningful reading experiences. Consequently, providing opportunities for teacher-led and peer discussions as well as individual reading reflections that teachers can explore with students one-on-one increases the possibility that reading can impact student life transitions. In addition, teachers may want to hold parent information sessions or host evenings during which family members can receive tips and ask questions about reading and discussing books with their middle school students as, far too often, family reading is abandoned when the elementary grades end.

Consolidating Identity

Good quality books assist in the consolidation of adolescents' identity by providing literary role models that may be missing in students' real lives. A skillful teacher can introduce characters—either fictional or historical—who illustrate traits adolescents may need to develop or traits they already possess but not yet recognize within themselves.

Drawing out these powerful attributes through activities that specifically ask students to compare themselves to characters (e.g., their strengths, challenges, problem-solving strategies, and insights) can bolster their resilience through identification of positive internal assets. As a student named Caden says, "I never thought about how really strong I had been until I read 'Tiger Eyes' and then I saw that other kids lose a parent, too, but they survive, and no matter how depressed they feel and how sad they are, they can find a way to get through it later on."

This identity building can be amplified in books that provide all the experiences mentioned earlier, but they also help students consolidate racial, ethnic, gender, or religious identity. Rather than relegating the use of books that derive from specific cultures to celebrations, holidays, or dedicated months (such as Black History Month), consciously choosing diverse literature for classroom use and for individual reading assignments as well as deliberately presenting assignments that help students identify the universal and the unique in the literary characters can aid in identity consolidation during the middle school years.

Breaking Down Stereotypes

Because middle school students have entered a period in which social confor-
mity can be highly prized, a primary task of social education at this level is to
inculcate the value of viewing people as individuals, not stereotypes. In
recent years, authors and publishers have become increasingly sensitive to
this issue, and they avoid stereotyping along all lines. While gender and
racial stereotypes have been discussed more prevalently, a new breed of
adolescent literature tackles the more subtle stereotypes associated with disability, age, social class, family configuration, and sexual orientation.

Students whose life circumstances may put them "outside the norms" of
the school or community in which they live cannot fully identify with literature unless they encounter characters who also may find themselves in the
margins. In addition, "majority" students cannot fully develop empathy and
social advocacy unless they are sensitized to others' realities. Often, literature can provide a more comfortable vehicle for these exchanges.

Eighth-grader Tasha sums this concept up by reflecting on reading books
in which characters faced bullying and homelessness: "I haven't ever really
had to go through anything really bad myself, so it was kind of sad to think
about what it would be like to not have a house or have to live in a shelter
with other people. We all know kids who are picked on, and I guess that me
and my friends are going to have to be more brave to not let that happen to
kids who aren't popular."

Motivating Marginalized Readers

Norton (2013) points out educators largely emphasize the "aesthetic approach" to literature in the classroom, allowing students to identify with the
characters and topics in the texts. To do this successfully, a teacher must be
able to "connect students with literary work through discussions that link
students' background knowledge, personal interests, and responses" (Norton,
2013, p. 36). Because middle school teachers tend to be of majority culture
and female, they may be less well versed in providing inclusive materials to
entice the marginalized reader.

As an eighth-grade boy comments, "Now I like to read more about real
things, like sports and heroes and kids that are having real problems but they
figure out how to solve them, you know. . . . Not so much the kind of stuff
that teachers give us to read." Another student shares that "we can pick pretty
much what we want to read when it is free reading time, but when the teacher
picks a book for the whole class to study, it's usually more about what girls
are interested in—like family stuff and emotional stuff—than what boys like
to read."

Given the social nature of middle school, it makes sense to set reading activities in an interpersonal context as well as an individualized one. Reading with partners, reading in small groups, creating blogs, and other means of sharing reading through posts or exchanging journals connects young readers with one another and creates excitement.

As Katie mentions, "Our teacher had us share our reading journals in small groups, and we could write to each other and make comments about what the other person had said. Sometimes we just all were agreeing about a certain character or what was going on, but sometimes someone else had written something that you just never thought of before!"

Some schools have found success in using mentors to promote reading activities. This support can be particularly effective if "cool" older students serve as reading mentors to middle schoolers. Not only does the interaction strengthen literacy skills and model the pleasure in reading, but it also provides students with additional social connections, greater esteem, and broader inclusion in the life of the school community.

Addressing the Gender Gap in Reading

By the middle school grades, a serious gap in reading achievement exists between boys and girls. Jacobsen (2014) notes that the competitive curricula pushed by contemporary schools leave less-verbal boys behind as early as fourth or fifth grade and create an image in their minds that they are not as proficient in reading as girls are.

Jacobsen (2014) further points out that boys and girls approach reading "in fundamentally different ways," with girls enjoying relating to the books' characters and equating reading fiction with pleasure, while boys want immediate utility from what they read (p. 48). Boys want to see a point for what they are reading, and they need a real-world use for the text. Jacobsen (2014) characterizes middle school boys' reading interests as gravitating towards "magazines, graphic novels, and books that feature gory scenes or gross humor" (p. 4).

Jacobsen (2014) suggests several successful approaches to encouraging boys to read, including engaging dads or other valued males in literacy efforts, broadening the scope of what qualifies as appropriate reading material in the classroom, taking advantage of technology to motivate boys to read, and targeting topics of interest in research reading to gain applicable information. Websites such as GuysRead.org, GettingBoysToRead.com, and BoysRead.org contain a wealth of useful, literacy-related information and reading suggestions for educators and parents.

CONCLUSION

Identity formation, and its myriad related tasks, occupies much of the developmental energy of adolescents. Quality literature written for this age group is a valuable tool for teachers and parents, as they assist middle school students in navigating the transition from childhood to adolescence. But to reach them, especially those who are reluctant readers, one must search for literature featuring characters that face similar developmental challenges and struggles as they do.

Making connections with characters who are successful in solving their problems and who display positive attributes that empower others provides more than literary skills; it provides role models for life. The notion of what is "acceptable reading material" in schools must be reconfigured to include those materials that entice the marginal reader. If middle school students are able to see a purpose for their reading and also see themselves in the characters in chosen texts, they are far more likely to become lifelong readers who value the printed word and seek out the rewards that regular reading can provide.

POINTS TO REMEMBER

- Meaningful reading experiences can foster pro-social development among middle school students.
- Teachers must have intimate knowledge of the students in their classrooms to be able to select books that address the students' developmental needs.
- Because adolescents identify with characters in books, teachers can use quality literature to illustrate how those characters solve problems, overcome challenges, and effect change in their environments.
- Educators must adopt deliberate strategies to help students recognize that they share the personal assets and strengths demonstrated by literary characters.
- Boys and girls have different styles and interests in reading, and teachers should recognize these distinctions when planning a classroom literature program.
- Recognizing the diversity of students within contemporary classrooms, teachers need to reflect that diversity in the choices of reading materials used in whole-class activities and free reading.
- Reading mentors can strengthen both literacy skills and social inclusion for marginalized readers.

REFERENCES

Benard, B. (1993). Fostering resiliency in kids. Educational Leadership, 51 (3), 44–48.
Brighton, K. (2007). Coming of age: The education and development of young adolescents. Westerville, OH: National Middle School Association.
Brooks, R., & Goldstein, S. (2004). The power of resilience. New York, NY: McGraw-Hill.
Brown, B., & Klute, C. (2004). Adolescent relationships with peers. In R. Lerner & L. Steinberg (Eds.), Handbook of adolescent psychology (pp. 363–94). New York, NY: Wiley.
Brown, D. F., & Knowles, T. (2007). What every middle school teacher should know. Portsmouth, NH: Heinemann.
Caissy, G. A. (1994). Early adolescence. Cambridge, MA: Perseus.
Erikson, E. H. (Ed). (1963). Youth: Change and challenge. New York: NY. Basic Books.
Gay, G. (1994). Coming of age ethnically: Teaching young adolescents of color. Theory into Practice, 33 (3), 149–55.
Henderson, N., & Milstein, M. (1996). Resiliency in schools: Making it happen. Thousand Oaks, CA: Corwin.
Holcomb-McCoy, C. (2014). Ethnic identity development in early adolescence: Implications and recommendations for middle school counselors. The Free Library. Retrieved from http://www.thefreelibrary.com/Ethnic+identity+development+in+early+adolescence%3a+implications+and...-a0140524755.
Jacobsen, L. (2014). Why boys don't read. Retrieved from http://www.greatschools.org/students/academic-skills/6832-why-so-many-boys-do-not-read.gs.
Kegan, R. (1982). *The evolving self: Problem and process in human development*. Cambridge, MA: Harvard Press.
Kroger, J. (2007). Identity development: Adolescence through adulthood. Thousand Oaks, CA: Sage.
Marcia, J. (1980). Identity in adolescence. In J. Adelson (Ed.), Handbook of adolescent psychology (pp. 159–87). New York, NY: Wiley.
Maslow, A. H. (1968). Toward a psychology of being. New York, NY: Van Nostrand Reinhold.
Norton, D. E. (2013). Multicultural children's literature: Through the eyes of many children. Boston, MA: Pearson.
Norton, D. E., & Norton, S. (2011). Through the eyes of a child: An introduction to children's literature. Boston, MA: Pearson.
Phinney, J. (1989). Stages of ethnic identity development in minority group adolescents. *Journal of Early Adolescence*, 9, pp. 34-49.
Pollack, W. S. (1998). Real boys: Rescuing our sons from the myths of boyhood. New York, NY: Henry Holt.
Rice, R. P., & Dolgin, K. G. (2005). The adolescent: Development, relationships, and culture. Boston, MA: Pearson.

Chapter Three

Cracking the Middle School Code

Characteristics of Effective Reading Programs

Sandra Donah

All parents dream of the day that their child will come home from school with a book in hand, waving it excitedly because he or she can read it independently, making his or her parents proud. For many parents, this dream becomes a reality when their child is in kindergarten. For some, that day takes another year or two to come true. For others, it may never come. The effects of continued reading difficulties can be devastating and life changing for students as they progress to middle school.

Learning to read is both one of the most fundamental and the most complicated tasks children must undertake during their early school years. Children enter school with the appropriate competencies to speak because spoken language is innate and does not have to be taught. Spoken language takes place at a preconscious level and is effortless (Shaywitz, 2003). Reading, however, is not a natural process; rather, it is a skill that must be acquired.

CHARACTERISTICS OF EFFECTIVE BEGINNING READING INSTRUCTION

The past fifteen years have produced extensive research on the most effective methods for teaching children to read. Snow, Burns, and Griffin (1998) identified and summarized the available literature on the skills necessary for children to learn to read at proficient levels. The National Reading Panel (2000) indicated that there were five major areas necessary for success in teaching reading: (1) phonemic awareness, (2) phonics, (3) text comprehension, (4) fluency, and (5) vocabulary instruction. The National Reading Panel

(2000) argued that instruction featuring all components in the regular education classroom is the best way to prevent reading disabilities in children.

THE READING CRISIS WITH MIDDLE AND HIGH SCHOOL STUDENTS

Despite clear evidence on the type of instruction necessary for students to
learn to read and the widespread expectation that all students can succeed
with appropriate instruction, America's education system continues to experience a crisis: middle and high school students are struggling to "break the
reading code," so to speak. The distressing ramifications for these struggling
students affect all areas of their lives. According to Joshi et al. (2009), more
than three thousand students drop out of school every day, and poor reading
and writing skills are cited as a factor.

In studies supported by the National Institute of Child Health and Human
Development, half of the students who have a criminal record and a history
of substance abuse problems have difficulties with reading (McCardle &
Chhabra, 2004). Approximately 33 percent of fourth graders and 25 percent
of eighth graders are reading below the basic level, which means that they are
having difficulty performing at minimum expectations for academic tasks
(Washburn, Joshi, & Cantrell, 2010).

These statistics suggest that direct reading instruction should continue
beyond the elementary years and should focus on the types of complex
literacy needs and weaknesses of the struggling students. Adolescent readers
who struggle "differ significantly from one another in their levels of reading
difficulty, but they also differ from one another in the nature of their reading
problems" (Torgesen et al., 2007, p. 67).

Some children have weaknesses with phonological processing and speed
and accuracy of word reading that must be addressed and meet the criteria of
having a specific learning disability, such as dyslexia. Other students can
decode and read fluently and effortlessly, but they lack the ability to comprehend or make connections in the text. Still others have weaknesses in both
word reading and comprehension. Adding to their difficulties in reading,
struggling readers face the demanding expectations of reading grade level
text in the content areas, which causes greater frustration and often loss of
hope (Torgesen et al., 2007).

The good news is that it is not too late to intervene for those older
students who struggle with the process of reading. Explicit, systematic,
multisensory instruction in the components of literacy where a particular
learner's weakness lies can close the achievement gap and help that student
break the reading code. Unfortunately, while middle school teachers realize
that many of their students are deficient in literacy skills, many lack the

practical knowledge required to teach the components of reading, as this task is assumed to be an elementary teacher's job (Kamil, 2003). Consequently, this chapter will delineate the components of reading instruction in the middle grades and emphasize the areas where older students might experience difficulty.

MOTIVATION

Before delving into the components of reading instruction, the effects of motivation on reading must be discussed. Motivation appears to play an important role in adolescents' reading skills. "It is often viewed as one of the determiners of adolescent literacy" (Kamil, 2003). Many factors affect a student's motivation in reading, including his or her goal for reading a text, having a choice in what text to read, the ability to collaborate with peers, and how interesting they find the content (Torgesen et al., 2007). Students who feel successful in a task are more motivated to learn.

When adolescents struggle with reading, there is a natural decline in motivation, as they see themselves compared to their peers in relation to their abilities (National Institute for Literacy, 2007). If teachers are going to succeed in instructing struggling reading students, then they must find ways to motivate them, especially since many of the concepts these students lack were taught early on in elementary school. Research indicates that without student motivation and engagement in this reading partnership, there will be no benefit from the instruction (Kamil, 2003).

DECODING

When students reach middle school, little thought is given to the need for instruction in phonemic awareness or phonics because this skill set is usually mastered by age five or six. Children who begin school with a decent understanding of phonological awareness have a better sense of how sounds and letters work together in words, which helps them make the connection between sounds and letters and prepares them to learn to read. In fact, phonemic awareness skills and letter knowledge are the single best predictors of reading success in first grade and beyond (National Reading Panel, 2000).

During the first three grades of elementary school, teachers largely focus on the sounds of the English language. Phonics involves the ability to recognize that sounds link to letters and those letters link to words, and it is the basic premise of the alphabetic principle, which allows for reading and spelling after students have mastered the sound-symbol associations in the English language.

Things shift in middle school from decoding individual phonemes in words to analyzing morphemes, which are the smallest units of meaning in words. These meaningful units are prefixes, suffixes, roots, and combining forms (Henry, 2003). The study of morphemes is especially helpful to middle school students, as content vocabulary often derives from Latin roots and Greek combining forms. Shaywitz (2003) contends that "knowing the etymology of the roots of a word is a very powerful aid to reading, shedding light on a word's pronunciation, its spelling, and its meaning" (p. 52).

Adolescent students benefit from direct instruction in morpheme patterns. For example, when students are taught the meaning of Latin roots, they then have the opportunity to see what other words can be built from that same morphemic unit, thus building vocabulary. Being aware of morphemic boundaries in a word, such as prefix, root, and suffix, can help students to decode more fluently and to build vocabulary (Kirk & Gillon, 2009). Teachers can provide direct instruction on how to unpack difficult words in text by separating the prefix, root, and suffix to help students derive meaning from unknown words and increase fluent decoding.

Morphemic instruction plays a vital role in supporting decoding, spelling, vocabulary, and comprehension. It offers a wonderful opportunity for content-area teachers to use word origins to assist students in understanding otherwise complex vocabulary and concepts. Students should be supported in attaining an awareness of morphemic structures in the English language, as research indicates that by fifth grade, morphological awareness is a stronger predictor of reading success than phonological awareness (Mann & Singson, 2003).

Older students who struggle with decoding present with the same difficulties as younger students; that is, they demonstrate poor decoding skills, use poor spelling, mispronounce words, and have difficulty remembering new words. Essentially, they lack phonemic awareness skills. Middle school students who struggle may not have internalized the sounds of the language and cannot readily associate a letter with its sound, nor can they spell accurately and effortlessly, which impacts their willingness to read and write in a classroom full of successful students.

When struggling students are faced with multisyllabic words, they lack the necessary skills to unpack the complex terms by seeing the prefix, suffix, and base as separate units. Due to these factors, struggling middle schoolers might attempt to decode this word by sounding out each individual phoneme rather than by looking for morphemic units.

FLUENCY

Thanks to research by the National Reading Panel (2000) and because of growing concern regarding students' dysfluent reading, fluency became one of the major components of an effective reading program. Fluency is defined as accurate reading at an appropriate rate with good expression and deep understanding (Hudson, Mercer, & Lane, 2000). When a student reads fluently, it is as if he or she is speaking. There is accuracy in the reading, with appropriate speed, phrasing, and expression, supporting comprehension of the text. Fluency is key because it builds the bridge between word recognition and comprehension.

Strong reading comprehension demands the fluent reading of words. Skilled readers rapidly recognize words and activate meaning, which in turn facilitates comprehension. Adams (1990) argues that "the automaticity with which skillful readers recognize words is the key to the whole system. The reader's attention can be focused on the meaning and message of a text only to the extent that it's free from fussing with the words and letters" (p. 414). Dysfluent readers must attend to the demands of attempting to decode words, thus losing the ability to gain meaning from the words they are reading.

In addition, as students move to middle school, classroom texts transition from more basic narrative text to more challenging expository text structures. Expository text features numerous content-area words that are multisyllabic, which may influence the prosody and fluency of text reading. Students' fluency can vary according to the type and content of text they are expected to read as well as the difficulty level of the text itself.

According to Reutzel and Cooter (2003), several strategies should be applied in a classroom to assist students in improving their fluency skills. Teachers should demonstrate what fluent and dysfluent reading sounds like. When students are exposed to appropriate and inappropriate models of reading, they gain an ear for what good reading should sound like. Although students are in middle school, educators should not back away from modeling quality reading practices.

Repeated readings are another strategy supported by research (Hasbrouk, Ihout, & Rogers, 1999). Practice with various text types provides students with experience and exposure to tackle difficult text while working on accurate reading and appropriate phrasing. Explicit instruction in fluency with feedback and guidance is an effective way to support students as they work on developing the skills necessary to become fluent readers.

For students who struggle with fluency, a major difficulty is their ability to decode words quickly. Rather than automatically recognizing words in the text, these students repeatedly sound out words as they read. This delayed decoding interferes with their ability to read smoothly, and it affects their comprehension because all their attention is spent deciphering the words instead of gaining meaning from the text (Adams, 1990).

Fluency remains an essential component to a comprehensive reading program, but again, it is not the only component. As previously mentioned, students who are able to read fluently do not have to focus all their attention on decoding skills, allowing them to better attend to the meaning of the text and to make text to text, text to self, and text to world connections. As such, fluency is integrally related to another component of reading: comprehension.

VOCABULARY

The importance of vocabulary knowledge and its role in reading has been known since the 1920s when Whipple (1925) contended that growth in word knowledge was directly related to growth in reading. Vocabulary knowledge is intricately intertwined with reading comprehension. As students read, they must know what most of the words in the text mean in order to comprehend the text as a whole. Students use their oral vocabulary to support their understanding of written text, and if they do not understand some vocabulary as they read, they must use strategies to help them gain understanding. The larger a reader's vocabulary, the easier it will be to gain meaning from text and make connections to the world around him or her.

Research indicates that certain vocabulary development strategies are more effective for adolescents. One supported strategy is preteaching difficult vocabulary (National Reading Panel, 2000). Direct instruction of specific vocabulary should include specific word instruction across contexts as well as strategies for learning new words. When specific words are taught before reading texts, vocabulary increases and comprehension improves as well. Vocabulary instruction is most effective when learning occurs over an extended period of time with multiple exposures to the vocabulary (Birsh, 2005).

Many researchers have debated how to decide which words to teach directly. Beck, McKowen & Kucan (2013) argue that vocabulary words fall into three tiers, with Tier 1 words being terms students encounter on a daily basis, Tier 2 words being terms found in literature, and Tier 3 terms being complex words found in content texts.

Tier 1 words do not need explicit instruction because they are encountered often and most children understand the meanings of these words. Tier 3 words are technical words found in subject matter materials, such as mathematics and science content, and are best learned in context as students encounter them. Tier 2 words, however, offer the best opportunity for direct instruction, as these words are used across contexts in literature during the students' school experiences.

Older struggling readers can face many challenges with vocabulary development. First, if word identification is problematic, students will certainly have difficulty decoding content-area words, especially those that are multisyllabic. Struggling students have not read as many words as grade-level peers, and as a result of this lack of reading practice, they have had less exposure to words and therefore might not yet have a given word in their print vocabulary (Kamil, 2003). Students also might not have an adequate understanding of how to learn unknown words by using morphemic structures (Henry, 2003). Lacking an understanding in the multiple meanings of many words affects students' ability to derive the meaning of an unfamiliar term in context (National Institute for Literacy, 2007).

Vocabulary instruction plays an important role in reading comprehension, and teachers and parents can support vocabulary building through multiple means. Vocabulary can grow through indirect opportunities via conversation with parents and teachers. In the classroom, educators can enhance vocabulary growth through active engagement of students in multiple exposures to new words across contexts. This development of word consciousness will pay huge dividends by helping students to not only improve their knowledge of words but boost their reading comprehension as well.

COMPREHENSION

The ultimate goal of literacy is to gain meaning from written content, and comprehension instruction plays an essential role in students' abilities to gain meaning and make connections effectively. Skilled adolescent readers read with a purpose in mind, are strategic, and think critically to support their understanding of text (Kamil, 2003).

Most people see reading as two separate entities based on the age level of the student: from kindergarten through grade three, students learn to read, while in grades four through high school, the purpose is reading to learn (Chall, 1996). This common mindset appears to imply that by the time a student is in third grade, he or she has mastered the skills of reading, and there is nothing left to learn when it comes to literacy. Further, according to this view, students will use those skills to learn in academic subjects such as science, social studies, and mathematics.

Current research, however, indicates that adolescent students need continued explicit instruction in reading to make additional progress in understanding more complex texts, and this instruction should be sustained until they graduate from high school if they are to leave school proficient in reading (Torgesen et al., 2007).

For middle school students, the explicit instruction of comprehension strategies across all content areas should become a larger focus. Research indicates that comprehension among adolescents can be improved through the instruction of just a few comprehension strategies: comprehension monitoring, graphic organizers, story structure, questioning, and summarization (National Institute for Literacy, 2007; National Reading Panel, 2000).

Comprehension monitoring, whose purpose is to help students become strategic, metacognitive readers, can be achieved by teaching students steps to monitor their comprehension and steps they must take to fix reading difficulties as they arise. Strong readers know when they understand what they have read and when they do not. They also have strategies in place to fix problems when reading does not make sense.

Teachers provide instruction that helps students become aware of their thinking as they read, enabling them to identify specifically what they do not understand so that they can resolve the problem and keep reading. Comprehension monitoring is a mental process, and it is impossible for teachers to see inside the heads of their students, but when teachers verbally read text aloud and model their thinking, it allows students to "see" the proper thought processes in action.

Another recognized strategy with positive effects for adolescents is graphic organizers, which are visual representations that facilitate ways to organize information and thoughts for understanding, remembering, or writing. Graphic organizers help readers focus on the structural elements of the text as well as how concepts are related within the text. Graphic organizers can be used for both expository and narrative text structures.

When middle school students are taught to use graphic organizers for expository text, it helps them understand varying text structure categories. For example, a graphic organizer for a cause-and-effect passage looks considerably different than a graphic organizer for a descriptive passage. When students know how to use the various organizers they have been taught, it supports their understanding and knowledge of challenging concepts in science and social studies.

Story structure is a third strategy with evidence to support its use in classrooms. Story structure provides a framework for identifying story elements in narrative texts, including characters, setting, problem, plot, and resolution. Research indicates that instruction in story structure improves students' ability to understand a story, answer questions, and remember what they have read (National Reading Panel, 2000).

Questioning is another supported comprehension strategy. Proficient readers ask themselves questions as they read. To have an impact on comprehension, students must be taught specific models of questioning that can be used before, during, and after reading. Two types of questioning that evidence best practice are question answering and question generating.

In question answering, teachers instruct students about the different types of questions, such as those whose answers can be found in the text and those that require background knowledge and experience to answer. In question generating, teachers instruct students about how to ask themselves questions while they read as a way of self-monitoring comprehension and how to fix any difficulties if they should arise.

Summarization is a complex strategy that requires students to focus on the main idea in the paragraph or text while weeding out irrelevant details. Students must then restate the information in their own words. This process is difficult for most students without explicit instruction, but when students eventually master the steps required to summarize a text, there are positive effects in generalizing to other texts and improving comprehension.

The strategies highlighted in this chapter have yielded effective results when used individually, but research findings also suggest that students benefit when multiple strategies are used simultaneously to aid comprehension (National Reading Panel, 2000). When students use multiple strategies such as prediction, questioning, comprehension monitoring, and summarization, their ability to comprehend text is the most effective. Skilled readers must be flexible in their thinking and able to repair difficulties as they occur so that their text comprehension is not impeded.

For many older struggling students, accessing grade-level text is especially difficult at the middle school level. Not only do they struggle to decode multisyllabic words, but their lack of fluency negatively impacts their understanding of text. Because these students have not read as many books as their peers, their vocabulary knowledge is likely to be lower, which of course affects their reading comprehension skills.

As mentioned elsewhere, the text structure of middle school academic content differs substantially from that of earlier grades. Science, social studies, and history materials utilize expository text structure, which struggling students are not familiar with, and these learners often do not understand the comprehension strategies best utilized with expository text (National Institute for Literacy, 2007).

CONCLUSION

Skilled reading is a complex process, even more so for adolescent students during their middle school years. During this time in an adolescent's life, motivation towards reading can falter, so teachers must find ways to motivate students and enable them to use strategies and engage the text to support their comprehension (Torgesen et al., 2007). No longer is it exclusively the English language arts teacher's responsibility to instruct students in the components of reading.

To assist students in becoming proficient readers, content teachers must now accept the responsibility of using their particular content area to instruct students in comprehension strategies that are relevant to their discipline, along with introducing vocabulary in multiple exposures. It is a daunting job, but with professional development and a commitment from the school community, educators can assist students in becoming independent, purposeful, critical thinkers, ready for the postsecondary world of work or education.

For those readers who struggle, explicit instruction in the specific areas of weakness is imperative to closing the achievement gap and solving the reading crisis for America's middle and high school students. Educators must continue to use current research on the components of reading instruction to broaden their knowledge base on the most effective methods for teaching literacy. When teachers use this knowledge to drive their instruction, they can intervene and prevent students from failing to learn how to read adequately. Effective instruction can stop the devastating social, emotional, and academic realities that struggling readers face every day.

POINTS TO REMEMBER

- Statistics confirm the need for direct reading instruction beyond the elementary years to focus on the complex literacy needs and weaknesses of struggling middle and high school readers.
- Because motivation plays a critical role in adolescents' reading skills, teachers must find a way to engage and motivate students who are struggling.
- Adolescent students benefit from direct instruction in morpheme patterns (i.e., prefixes, roots, combining forms, and suffixes) to support the more complex decoding, vocabulary, and comprehension of text read in middle and high school.
- It is imperative that content-area teachers instruct students to think using comprehension strategies from their discipline, along with introducing vocabulary in multiple exposures.
- Teachers must use current research on the five components of reading to broaden their knowledge base on the most effective methods of teaching reading to all students.

REFERENCES

Adams, M. (1990). Beginning to read: Thinking and learning about print. Cambridge, MA: MIT Press.
Beck, I. L., McKeown, M.G., & Kucan, L. (2013). Bringing words to life. 2nd ed. New York, NY: Guilford Press.

Birsh, J. (Ed.) (2005). Multisensory teaching of basic language skills. 2nd ed. Baltimore, MD: Paul Brookes Publishing

Chall, J. (1996). Learning to read: The great debate. 3rd ed. Fort Worth, TX: Harcourt Brace.

Foorman, B. R., & Moats, L. C. (2004). Conditions for sustaining researched based practices in early reading instruction. Remedial and Special Education, 25 (1), 51–60.

Hasbrouk, J., Ihout, C., & Rogers, G. (1999). Read naturally: A strategy to increase oral reading fluency. Reading Research and Instruction, 39, 27–37.

Henry, M. (2003). Unlocking literacy: Effective decoding and spelling instruction. Baltimore, MD: Brookes.

Hudson, R. F., Mercer, C. D., & Lane, H. B. (2000). Exploring reading fluency: A paradigmatic overview. Unpublished manuscript. University of Florida, Gainesville.

Joshi, R., Binks, E., Hougen, M., Dahlgren, M., Ocker-Dean, E., & Smith, D. (2009). Why elementary teachers might be inadequately prepared to teach reading. Journal of Learning Disabilities, 42 (5), 392–402.

Kamil, M. (2003). Adolescents and literacy: Reading for the 21st century. Washington, DC: Alliance for Excellent Education.

Kirk, J., & Gillon, K. (2009, July 1). Morphology and literacy: Getting our heads in the game. Language, Speech, and Hearing Services in Schools, 40 (3), 283–85.

Mann, V. & Singson, M. (2003). Linking morphological knowledge to English decoding ability: Large effects of little suffixes. In E. Assink & D. Sandra (Eds), *Reading complex words: Cross- language studies* (pp. 1-25). New York, NY: Kluwer Academic/Plenum Publishers, pp. 1-2.

McCardle, P., & Chhabra, V. (2004). The voice of evidence in reading research. Baltimore, MD: Brookes.

National Institute for Literacy. (2007). What content-area teachers should know about adolescent literacy. Washington, DC: National Institute for Literacy, National Institute for Child Health and Human Development, U.S. Department of Education's Office for Vocational and Adult Education.

National Reading Panel. (2000). Teaching students to read: Evidence-based assessment of the scientific research literature on reading and its implications for reading instruction. Bethesda, MD: National Reading Panel, National Institute of Child Health and Human Development.

Reutzel, D., & Cooter, R. (2003). Strategies for reading instruction assessment: Every child a successful reader. Upper Saddle River, NJ: Merrill/Prentice-Hall.

Shaywitz, S. (2003). Overcoming dyslexia: A new and complete science-based program for reading problems at any level. New York, NY: Knopf.

Snow, C., Burns, M., & Griffin, P. (Eds.). (1998). Preventing reading difficulties in young students. Washington, DC: National Academy Press.

Torgesen, J. K., Houston, D. D., Rissman, L. M., Decker, S. M., Roberts, G., Vaughn, S., Wexler, J., Francis, D. J., Rivera, M. O., & Lesaux, N. (2007). Academic literacy instruction for adolescents: A guidance document from the Center on Instruction. Portsmouth, NH: RMC Research Corporation, Center on Instruction.

Washburn, E., Joshi, R., & Cantrell, D. (2010). Are pre-service teachers prepared to teach struggling readers? Annals of Dyslexia, 1–23.

Whipple, G. (Ed.). (1925). The 24th yearbook of the National Society for the Study of Education: Report of the National Committee on Reading. Bloomington, IL: Public School Publishing Company.

Chapter Four

Reading and the Brain

Using Neuroscience to Improve the Reading Process

Toni Spinelli-Nannen and Roberta Green

Reading is one of the most researched areas in education, and tremendous emphasis has been placed on the development of reading skills. Perhaps this is because reading ability is necessary to access all areas of the curriculum. Perhaps it is because schools have attempted many types of interventions that have not proven efficacious, and there is a need to learn more.

Whatever the reason, more is known now than ever before about the foundational skills necessary to learn to read, how phonological skills and fluency develop, and the underlying deficits that hinder reading fluency and reading comprehension among students. For children who are typical readers, almost any method will work, and they will learn to read. However, for children with an underlying learning disability in reading, it is important to understand their learning difficulties and to use specific strategies and interventions.

Currently, educators are able to proceed confidently with very young children. Research shows that they need a structured, sequential, explicit approach in developing phonological decoding skills, fluency, vocabulary, and reading comprehension. Progress is measurable.

For older children and adolescents, the picture is not as clear. What works? What does not work? Should educators continue to teach phonics to older students? Why do some middle and high school students not make progress even with intensive special education supports in place?

Surprisingly often, middle and high school students have an incomplete mastery of phonology decoding, a poor vocabulary, and lack of fluency when reading. Because the ultimate purpose for reading is understanding, a lack of foundation skills significantly impacts reading and learning in the content areas. Perhaps the answer lies, at least partially, in the brain systems that are the very basis of language and reading.

LANGUAGE AND READING

While language appears to be an innate function of the human brain, it is experience that ensures a child will learn language with adequate exposure. Reading, on the other hand, is not innate and must be explicitly taught and learned. Language and reading, however, are intricately related with adequate language development setting the foundation for the learning of reading.

Language development in the preschool child is an excellent predictor of later reading ability. They need to play with language so that they develop an understanding that there is a connection between the words that are spoken and the marks on the paper. This, of course, suggests that talking to toddlers, reading to them, and asking them to describe situations will help solidify that foundation.

Language skills consist of the processes of reception (the detection, discrimination, and interpretation of spoken symbols) and expression (the production of spoken symbols). There are four areas of the dominant hemisphere that contribute to the reception and expression of language. Speech sounds are received through the ear and transmitted along the auditory nerve to the primary auditory cortex in the temporal lobe.

The interpretation and meaning of speech sounds involves Wernicke's area in the posterior portion of the superior temporal gyrus, while the organization of grammar and syntax for articulation of speech sounds involves Broca's area in the dominant inferior frontal gyrus. Therefore, Broca's area, which is near the motor control center of the brain, is involved in the production of speech sounds.

Articulation errors, word sequencing, and word retrieval difficulties are apparent with damage to Broca's area. Wernicke's area, which is far from the motor cortex, is involved in the understanding of language. Poor or incomprehensible content in the language used to communicate is apparent with damage to Wernicke's area, while articulation remains intact.

Given that neuroscience has provided a significant increase in knowledge about reading, it is possible to identify the cognitive skills underlying the reading process. This implies that it is possible to identify and understand when these skills are weak and what interventions can be designed and used in an educational setting for children and adolescents. By definition, at least average intelligence must be present for identification of a reading disability, but the issue is somewhat more complex, and a simple discrepancy between ability and achievement reveals very little.

Why, despite adequate instruction, motivation to succeed, and a supportive environment, do some children have difficulty learning to read? In general, specific difficulty with reading is a language problem, not a problem with intellectual ability or thinking skills. Because it certainly is not a problem with vision, the visual system, or the motor system, an overview of the brain systems involved in this language-based skill is of considerable value.

ORGANIZATION OF THE BRAIN FOR THE READING PROCESS

The brain is highly adaptable, allowing us to change behavior in response to the environment in which we find ourselves, thus ensuring survival. The process begins during prenatal development when there is an initial overproduction of neurons (the cells of the nervous system) and connections among neurons. At birth, the process of neural death, or apoptosis, begins leaving the brain with one hundred billion neurons and one hundred trillion synapses, or connections among neurons. These neurons have small branching structures called dendrites at one end of the cell body and long projections called axons at the other end of the cell body.

The axons of one neuron project to the dendrite of another neuron, making a connection. The axon and the dendrite do not actually touch, and there is a small space called a synapse between them. As the brain matures, there is a fatty sheath that develops around the axon, increasing the efficiency of the neural impulse. Myelination in most of the brain is not complete at birth, although there are areas in which almost complete myelination occurs, such as in the brain stem and the spinal cord (i.e., the areas of the central nervous system essential for life).

Subcortical areas, such as the thalamus, basal ganglia, some midbrain regions, and the cerebellum, which modulate sensory and motor function, develop during the first two years of life. The cortex and cortical areas responsible for complex thinking and problem solving as well as all higher-level cognitive processes take longer to develop. This is a developmental process. Neurons form connections with other neurons, and axons become myelinated to make the process of neural transmission more efficient, and the procedure is from basic functions first and more complex functions later.

Reading is a complex cognitive skill requiring that the brain receive information from multiple brain regions. It is an open-ended process, indicating that consistent environmental input is important in the formation of necessary neural connections. The genetic influence provides the basic prewiring and dictates the direction and growth of neurons and synapses. However, it is the experience that shapes and strengthens the functional capacity of these connections. The bottom line is that practice and repetition strengthen the neural connections required for proficient reading.

Interestingly, while experience strengthens the connections, lack of experience may diminish or even eliminate the connections. The general concept is that at birth, the brain is relatively hardwired for basic survival functions that are regulated in the spinal cord and the brain stem and relatively soft-wired for higher-level, complex functions such as reading.

To a great extent, environment and practice do not alter the brain processes that are hardwired, whereas environmental experience and practice change and strengthen brain processes that are softwired. Basically, the brain is biologically prepared for the experiences that will lead to the development of reading skills, but specific reading experiences and repetition of these experiences are essential to the development of automatic and efficient reading.

HOW READING STRENGTHENS NEURAL CONNECTIONS

As brain development progresses prenatally, neurons are guided to their final positions in the brain by cells that are called radial glial cells, fine stringlike structures that pull the neurons along, and a membrane stops the progression. These final positions are biologically predetermined, and neurons are in place by the sixth prenatal month (Kalat, 2013). Phonological processing takes place in the left hemisphere at the junction of the temporal and parietal lobes.

Activation has been reported in the left temporal parietal region and the plana temporal during tasks that require phonological processing, including rhyming, segmenting sounds, and blending the individual sounds in words. For adequate phonological processing to occur, the neurons or brain cells must be in their final position in these areas, and appropriate connections to other neurons must be established. If the neurons do not reach the predetermined destination in the brain, there is a cascading effect, and all other structures and functions will be compromised.

Reading is a unique task. Learning to read requires the creation of new neural connections and the reorganization of other neural connections. There is no innate word recognition center in the brain, so how do strong readers automatically and efficiently recognize words? In fact, it is impossible not to recognize a word and understand its meaning after automaticity has been established.

It is likely that automatic word recognition is progressively learned, beginning first by mastery of phonological decoding skill. The mastery of these phonetic skills forms the basis of a visual word form area in the brain that allows for automatic word recognition. Research findings strongly support the presence of specific neurons in the fusiform gyrus in the left hemisphere of the extrastriate cortex of the occipital lobes that is a visual word form area.

PROCESSING AND EXECUTIVE FUNCTION

Both visual processing and auditory processing, along with several important executive function skills, are involved in reading. Of course, learning to read is a process, and the initial stages of learning to read involve recognizing visual symbols. First, the visual system is involved in whole-word reading. Deficits in visual-perceptual processing may result in impaired whole word reading but unimpaired ability to sound out words.

Deficits in the auditory system may result in impaired ability to sound out words but unimpaired whole-word reading. Working memory, as one executive skill, regulates these two systems called the visuospatial sketchpad and the articulatory phonological loop. The phonological loop acts as a temporary buffer for holding and manipulating auditory and verbal information, and the visuospatial sketchpad is a temporary buffer for holding and manipulating visual and visual perceptual information (Feifer & Toffalo, 2007).

In addition, the impact of the visual system involves what is called flicker fusion, the speed at which two distinct visual images combine to form one image when the images are presented in quick succession. Two different cells in the visual system are part of this process as information is sent from the retina to the visual cortex. Magnocellular cells are the large cells located in the inferior region of the lateral geniculate bodies; they are highly responsive to movement, rapid stimulus change, low contrast, and spatial location.

Parvocellular cells are smaller cells located dorsally in the lateral geniculate bodies; they are responsive to stationary objects, color, high contrast, and fine spatial details. The magnocellular cells are activated during rapid eye movement, while the parvocellular cells are activated during eye fixation. During reading, brief fixations are separated by rapid eye movements called saccades.

The magnocellular system inhibits the parvocellular system at each saccade, ending the eye fixation. In dyslexia, the magnocellular system may not inhibit the parvocellular system so that the letters seen in one fixation blur into the next fixation. Even though the visual system is involved in reading, evidence suggests that it is the phonological loop that is correlated most strongly with skilled reading (Miller, 2010).

THE CONTRIBUTION OF PHONOLOGICAL DECODING SKILLS

It is now necessary to look at phonological decoding more closely. Phonological awareness refers to the ability to perceive and manipulate the smallest pieces of a language. In English, there are forty-four phonemes that represent speech sounds. It is important to distinguish between phonics knowledge, which is the former, and phonological awareness, which is the knowledge of sound patterns and what sounds are associated with what letters (i.e., grapheme-phoneme relationships).

For example, phonics knowledge is the ability to associate the sound /b/ with the letter *b*. However, phonological awareness refers to the ability to manipulate the sounds in an efficient manner. For example, phonological awareness is the ability to hear the sounds /b/, /a/, and /t/ and blend them together for the word *bat*. Conversely, it is also the ability to hear the word *bat* and be able to take out the sound /b/ and know that the remaining word is *at* (Adams, 1990). Areas of the left hemisphere of the brain are usually correlated with linguistic skills or language so that the plana temporale in the left hemisphere is larger than the plana temporale in the right hemisphere.

In the brains of children with reading disabilities, the plana temporale of the left hemisphere is equal in size to that of the right hemisphere. However, research indicates that this symmetry is caused not by the right side being larger but by the left side being smaller. Overall, the brains of individuals with dyslexia tend to be larger than those without dyslexia, and the two hemispheres are more symmetric (Hale & Fiorello, 2004).

The seminal work of Sally Shaywitz (2004) provides the relevant information to understand the brain process and the development of phonological awareness. Her work indicates that phonological development is only an intermediate step in the process of reading and that decoding skills allow for the mapping of highly complex synapses to be coded in the fusiform gyrus of the left hemisphere for the eventual automaticity of word reading.

A strong connection exists between phonological decoding skills and the acquisition of automatic word recognition skills. Any structural or functional disruption in the temporal parietal regions of the brain that are essential for the development of phonological processing may cause progressive difficulty in the formation of the specific neural connections in the visual word form area. If this occurs, specifically during critical periods of development, significant deficits in automatic word reading may be present.

THE CONTRIBUTIONS OF SPECIFIC EXECUTIVE FUNCTION SKILLS

As mentioned previously, working memory and attentional skills are often controlled by the executive function system (Hale & Fiorello, 2004). Executive skills are largely part of the prefrontal cortex, and they have served to improve adaptive behaviors in response to actual environmental situations. This is true of reading as well. Both visual and verbal working memories are important in the ability to automatically recognize words in print.

Difficulty with visual working memory impairs recognition of the orthography, or visual shape, of words; the result is inconsistency in recalling spelling rules (Feefer & Toffalo, 2007). Difficulty with auditory working memory hinders the ability to connect sounds in a word to the appropriate letters in the correct sequence; the result is inconsistency in sounding out the letters in a sequential manner.

The characteristics of vigilance and attention are required to organize productive speech, and the frontal lobe is responsible for these behaviors. However, attention is complicated and involves several different processes. First, focused attention is necessary to develop the ability to track words appropriately across lines of text without losing one's place. Second, sustained attention is necessary to read to the end of a paragraph, a passage, or a chapter. Third, shifting attention is required to change from one reading task to another. Fourth, divided attention is required to be in the process of reading a passage while listening to the teacher. Finally, attentional capacity is necessary to read a complex passage while keeping the information in mind.

While visual and verbal working memory and attentional skills are necessary for efficient reading, other executive function skills also play a part. These other executive function skills involve the ability to plan, organize, make decisions, solve problems, and initiate and coordinate behaviors. These executive functions are important in several areas of reading comprehension.

First, the ability to plan is necessary to read with a purpose. Second, organization is necessary to connect text for understanding. Third, cognitive flexibility is important to shift ways of thinking as the text changes. Fourth, concept formation is necessary to acquire a deep understanding of the text. Finally, response inhibition is important to refrain from jumping around when reading, which results in missing important information.

EFFECTIVE READING INSTRUCTION

The National Reading Panel (2000) provides a review of scientific research in the field and has established the guidelines for effective reading instruction. Four areas of literacy instruction have been identified: phonology, fluency, vocabulary, and comprehension. For children, instructional emphasis is on phonological decoding skills. For adolescents, the emphasis is on comprehension. If phonology has not been addressed early in the process of language and reading development, it becomes increasingly difficult to establish brain-based changes. However, it is important to continue to teach reading to middle school students while they begin to read to learn.

For children, there are several important points. In general, phonological awareness programs have been successful. However, explicit and intense training procedures are usually required to have a substantial effect on the phonological awareness in students who are having difficulty developing these skills. To enhance the effectiveness of phonological awareness, several characteristics of instruction are important to consider.

Educators ought to focus first on the auditory features of words, then move from the explicit and natural segments of language to the more implicit and complex. The phonological properties and dimensions of words need to be used to enhance performance and scaffold blending segments through explicit modeling. Finally, letter-sound correspondence should be integrated after learners are proficient with auditory tasks.

Fluency is the ability to read quickly and accurately, and it is a critical component of an effective reading program. Fluency instruction should occur across several skill areas: phonemic awareness, letter naming, sound-letter associates, sight words, and oral reading of connected text. This type of instruction often requires repeated practice with the same information so that fluency increases in increments.

Vocabulary refers to the words a person has learned and uses to communicate effectively, and it is generally divided into oral vocabulary (both listening and speaking) and reading vocabulary. Most words are learned indirectly through daily experience with written and oral language, making repeated exposure to literature and guided discussion essential. Reading aloud is helpful, especially if the reader pauses to discuss new words. These processes can be guided by adults or more competent peers. Conversations about a book or story enhance student learning of concepts and words.

In addition to discussion, difficult words should be taught directly with extended instruction of specific words over time and across different contexts to help with the generalization of words to different settings. Repeated exposure to target words should be provided along with information about word parts, such as prefixes, suffixes, root words, and base words (Moats, 2009). This not only helps with vocabulary development, but it also provides information for decoding. When paired with direct instruction, interventions that engage a student interactively with memory devices (such as mnemonics) and graphic depictions (such as semantic maps) appear most promising.

Comprehension is an active process that enables the learner to understand the words being read. In their zeal to teach phonics, educators often overlook the fact that comprehension is the reason for reading and that it requires purposeful, thoughtful interaction with text. Reading comprehension improves through explicit teaching of specific cognitive strategies. It is necessary to use strategic reasoning when encountering barriers to understanding while reading. Adult modeling of comprehension strategies is important until students can use them independently.

For adolescents, it is important to address decoding errors as they occur while the student is reading. Some decoding errors are the result of carelessness or impulsive responses. Even if the student knows the rules of decoding, it is important for the teacher to correct the errors because these types of errors tend to hinder comprehension. Notably, direct instruction in phonics out of context of content-area reading is usually not effective during adolescence.

Vocabulary also can be addressed through content. Teachers can determine if a student knows the basic meaning of a term by asking him or her to define the word clearly and explicitly. However, simply defining a word does not usually ensure that the student possesses an in-depth understanding and a readiness to use the word independently. Educators should use words in various situations and discuss how a word is similar to or different from comparable words, as this approach helps the student to unlock shades of meaning.

While automaticity in decoding words is essential for fluency, reading with expression is part of the process. Reading at an adequate pace with emphasis on some words and recognizing the function of syntax and punctuation are important. Although adults often read aloud to children, they deem it unimportant for adolescents. However, reading aloud helps to identify the type of expression that might be necessary, and it clarifies the importance of punctuation for stops, hesitations, or emphasis. To improve in this area, students should reread frequently.

Education professionals have long recognized the necessity of teaching comprehension strategies directly rather than leaving understanding to chance. Because content becomes more sophisticated as adolescents move from middle school to high school, several instructional strategies will improve comprehension.

Specialized or technical vocabulary as well as critical facts needed to understand what is about to be read should be pretaught. The context ought to be provided, and the focal points of the information need to be highlighted for students. The entire passage or chapter should be summarized before reading. If necessary, teachers can lower the level of comprehension to the word or phrase level, the sentence level, the passage level, and finally the chapter or story level (Miller, 2010).

After reading, post-teaching is important. Teachers can ask students to summarize what has been read in a clear manner that requires fewer words rather than more words. This approach demonstrates and clarifies understanding better than a long summary that is rambling and unclear. The students should prioritize the ideas of elements of the passage. The adult can then help the students make connections from the passage to other texts, to the world, and to themselves.

CONCLUSION

Reading is a complicated learned skill. Although the brain is genetically prepared for the establishment of reading skills, solid teaching in oral language skills provides a foundation; repeated experience is necessary; and structured, sequential instruction is essential. Reading involves multiple brain areas, including the language areas, the motor system, the auditory system, the visual system, and the higher-level functions regulated by the executive system in the prefrontal cortex.

A small number of children will learn to read regardless of the method of instruction; however, most students benefit greatly from a structured, sequential phonics-based method. The inclusion of quality, age-appropriate literature will provide a model of strong writing as well as a motivation for reading.

The earlier the intervention starts, the greater likelihood that brain connections supporting automatic reading will be made. When the brain changes structurally in response to practice, it changes functionally by observable improvement in reading. For adolescents, it is unlikely that practice will produce changes in the brain areas or brain connections that are responsible for reading. Nevertheless, overall improvement in reading will happen with repeated practice and guidance in content-area reading.

Phonological methods are more likely to work with challenging words by using the context of what middle school students are reading in their classes. Notably, adolescents can make progress with phonics practice in the context of academic reading, repeated reading of the same material for development of fluency, instruction and expansion in vocabulary, and specific instruction in comprehension strategies.

POINTS TO REMEMBER

Education professionals and parents should be familiar with the following:

- How a student's brain is organized to receive and integrate information from various brain areas
- How practice and experience are related to the development of solid reading skills
- How learning to read creates new neural connections so that strong readers automatically and efficiently recognize words
- The importance of the visuospatial sketchpad and the phonological loop in the brain when learning to read
- The importance of phonological decoding skills and the development of phonological awareness in learning to read

- The contribution of specific executive function skills, such as visual and verbal working memory and attention, related to the reading process
- The basics of quality reading instruction
- Schools must take an active role in disseminating information on the brain and its role in reading to parents and caregivers; such information must be presented in a user-friendly manner so that family members can reinforce what is taking place in the classroom.

REFERENCES

Adams, M. (1990). Beginning to read: Thinking and learning about print. Cambridge, MA: MIT Press.

Feifer, S., & Toffalo, D. (2007). Integrating RTI with cognitive neuropsychology: A scientific approach to reading. Middletown, MD: School Neuropsych Press.

Hale, J., & Fiorello, C. (2004). School neuropsychology: A practitioner's handbook. New York, NY: Guilford Press.

Kalat, J. (2013). Biological psychology. Belmont, CA: Wadsworth.

Moats, L. (2009). From speech to print: Essentials for teachers. Baltimore, MD: Brookes.

Miller, D. (Ed.). (2010). School neuropsychology: Guidelines for effective practice, assessment, and evidence-based intervention. Hoboken, NJ: Wiley.

National Reading Panel. (2000, April). Teaching children to read: An evidence based assessment of the scientific research literature on reading and its implications for reading instruction. Rockville, MD: National Institute of Child Health and Human Development.

Shaywitz, S. (2004). Overcoming dyslexia. New York, NY: Random House.

Chapter Five

The Fundamentals of Reading Disorders

Gaining Insight Into Causes and Effects

Frank E. Vargo, Nicholas D. Young, and Richard D. Judah

WHAT IS A READING DISABILITY?

Simply stated, a reading disability is a neurological impairment of a person's ability to read. A reading disability is not associated with intellectual limitations, and most people with reading disorders possess normal levels of intelligence. Research indicates that between 5 percent and 17 percent of children have reading disabilities (McCandliss & Noble, 2003).

Reading disabilities are commonly referred to as *dyslexia*, a term coined at the beginning of the twentieth century, when it was believed that the condition was caused by deficits in visual processing whereby words and letters were reversed and transposed (Lange & Thompson, 2006). The term now has a much wider range of meanings and refers to a spectrum of conditions that negatively affect reading ability. Thus, *reading disability* and *dyslexia* are terms that, for the most part, can be used interchangeably. The basic characteristic of a reading disorder is an impaired ability to read.

CAUSES OF READING DISORDERS

Children with language problems are more likely to have reading disorders. Research has demonstrated that there is a relationship between reading disorders and delays in expressive language, receptive language, or both (Crouch

& Dozier, 2011). Also, children with such difficulties in language and reading are more likely than other children to have behavioral problems both at school and at home. In schools, children with reading disorders are sometimes identified as having a language-based learning disability.

The precise neurological cause for the development of reading disorders has not been precisely established. Scientific research, however, does suggest that the brains of individuals with reading disorders are in some ways different than those of individuals without reading disorders. Biological research findings based on family studies also suggest that reading disorders are hereditary. Research has found eight specific genetic deficits among subjects with reading disorders (Birsch, 2005). Boys are likely to have significantly more reading problems than girls (Valdois, Bosse, & Tainturier, 2004).

TYPES OF READING DISABILITIES

Phonological Processing

Most children with reading problems have what is known as a phonological processing disability. Phonemes are the smallest units or segments of sound used to produce meaningful speech. The brain reduces words into phonemic units before a person can identify, comprehend, or recall them. Humans are not consciously aware of this process. Phonemes are blended into complete words heard without seams or breaks. For instance, the word *sat* seems like a single, unbroken sound, but it can be segmented or separated into three phonemic components.

The smallest unit of written language is called a grapheme, and it is essentially the use of visual symbols to represent spoken sounds, or phonemes. The act of reading demands that the reader recognize the visual sequence of letters in a certain order and pair it with the correct phonology. Persons with this kind of reading disorder cannot effectively associate the visually processed letters with their proper sounds.

Basically, phonological processing refers to an individual's skill in accurately hearing, discriminating, recognizing, and understanding the various parts of sound used in language (Vargo, Grosser, & Spafford, 1995). Phonological awareness is the ability to hear and understand the sound symbols that correspond to the words on a printed page, which is a critical component of early reading development (Rayner & Pollatsek, 1989). Phonological awareness is also referred to as linguistic awareness and phonemic awareness. Phonological awareness is an important indicator of future reading abilities and reading problems (Vargo, 1992; Wagner, Torgesen, & Rashotte, 1999).

When a proficient reader picks up the morning newspaper, he or she obviously does not "sound out" each word as it is encountered. To do so would be extremely tedious and slow, and it would severely encumber the overall reading process (Rayner & Pollatsek, 1989; Spafford & Grosser, 1996). An experienced and accomplished reader will sequentially scan each word and quite instantaneously recognize (and subsequently "read") that word.

This process is commonly referred to as word automaticity, and it describes one's ability to read "fluently." Of course, when an unfamiliar word is encountered, fluent readers may utilize their skills in "sounding out" to decode that word. Repetition of a new word, initially decoded, through repeated reading exposures will eventually encode, or "permanently store," the word in an individual's long-term memory (Ashcraft, 1989; Cohen, Eysenck, & LeVoi, 1986; Matlin, 1989; Schank, 1982; Wagner, Torgesen, & Rashotte, 1999).

After a word's visual features are permanently "stored" in memory, the act of automatically identifying (reading) that word is a process of retrieval of the stored visual memory of that word (Brady, Shankweiler, & Mann, 1983; Schank, 1982; Wiig, Zureich, & Chan, 2000). This retrieval actually involves a complicated interaction of neurological activities.

Processing Speed—Orthographic Processing

People who experience problems with orthographic processing have difficulty reading because their brains cannot efficiently process the direction and sequence of the written word. When individuals with orthographic processing disorders attempt to read, their brains have trouble "seeing" the direction and sequence of written language (Shaywitz, 2003).

Approximately 10 percent to 15 percent of struggling readers have this type of difficulty (Shaywitz, 2003). Readers with this type of disability are often accurate in word recognition and reading of text, but they have difficulty with speed of word identification and automatic recall of word spellings; their phonemic awareness and other phonological skills may be unimpaired (Moats & Tolman, 2009).

Comprehension Difficulties

Another kind of reading disability involves problems in language processing and visual reasoning. Typically, children who struggle with reading comprehension can read words and spell correctly. Rather, their difficulties with literacy are caused by disorders of social reasoning, abstract verbal reasoning, or language comprehension. A disability in reading comprehension is indicated by problems understanding the important ideas in reading passages. Comprehension deficits may involve difficulty in one or more of the following features:

- Identifying the main idea
- Recalling sequential facts
- Making inferences or interpreting what has been read

In many cases, those with reading comprehension problems can read aloud without difficulty, but they do not understand or remember what they have read. Fluency and phrasing are often impaired as well. Not surprisingly, individuals with comprehension issues often avoid reading and are distressed when called upon to do so. Reading comprehension problems significantly interfere with a wide range of academic areas (Logsdon, 2012).

In the earlier elementary grades, deficits in reading comprehension are often more difficult to detect than the other types of reading disabilities. It is not until late elementary school when academic demands change and become more complex that comprehension issues may become apparent. As noted earlier, children who have not had difficulty with word reading or spelling may show increased difficulty understanding text as well as demonstrating inferential thinking (Badian, 1999).

OTHER DIFFICULTIES ASSOCIATED WITH READING COMPREHENSION DEFICITS

Attention Deficit/Hyperactivity Disorder

It is important to note that reading comprehension difficulties are actually heterogeneous and may or may not reflect a specific reading disability (Ghelani, Sidhu, Jain, & Tannock, 2004). Some kinds of disorders or conditions interfere with reading but do not fall within the definition of a specific learning disability; nevertheless, they are still considered disabilities and require school-based interventions and strategies.

For example, children with attention deficit/hyperactivity disorder may have serious problems with reading comprehension that are not language based or characterized by a failure to acquire rapid, context-free, word identification skills (Stanovich & Siegel, 1994). Attention deficit/hyperactivity disorder is considered a developmental disorder, or health-related condition, characterized by difficulties with inattention, impulsivity, and hyperactivity (Barkley, 1997).

Sensory Deficits

Visual perceptual deficits in functional areas such as tracking and scanning may also interfere with the comprehension of text. For children with such conditions, the capacity for maintaining physical and mental energy to perform tasks often results in diminished attention, unusual fatigue, poor comprehension, and predisposition for error. Comprehension problems in this case are not secondary to a specific learning disability but to a sensory-based disorder, such as a vision problem, that may require medical intervention versus individualized instruction.

Auditory problems can seriously interfere with an individual's ability to analyze or make sense of information that is gained through auditory channels. This could involve problems with hearing acuity, such as deafness or being hard of hearing. Although deficits in auditory processing do not involve acuity (i.e., what is heard by the ear), they do affect how this information is interpreted or processed by the central nervous system. A central auditory processing disorder is one of numerous disorders that are characterized by the way the central nervous system processes auditory information (American Academy of Audiology, 2010).

A central auditory processing disorder may adversely impact not only speech and language development, but it also can affect all areas of learning, particularly reading and spelling. When classroom instruction relies primarily on spoken language, individuals with auditory processing disorders may have tremendous difficulty understanding the lesson or the directions (National Center for Learning Disabilities, 1999).

Emotional and Behavioral Issues

Many students with emotional and behavioral disorders exhibit significant deficiencies in reading (Coleman & Vaughn, 2000; Maughan, Pickles, Hagell, Rutter, & Yule, 1996). Their challenges in reading can be attributed primarily to their behavioral excesses and deficits. Also, the correlation between academic failure and behavioral and emotional problems is not one way; disruptive behavior and defiance seems to universally lead to academic failure.

Many students with emotional or behavioral disorders also have coexisting learning disabilities and language delays that augment or amplify their difficulties in achieving academic success (Glassberg, Hooper, & Mattison, 1999). The disruptive and defiant behavior of students with emotional and behavioral disorders usually leads to academic failure. This failure, in turn, is a precursor for further misconduct (Hallenbeck, Kauffman, & Lloyd, 1995).

Aggression and disruptive actions are not the only behavioral or emotional impediments to positive achievement and social adaptation. Children with internalized disorders such as anxiety, depression, and social withdrawal are often too involved and distracted because of their emotional states to participate academically, socially, or both; thus, their reading comprehension and other academic skills suffer significantly.

Socio-Environmental Issues

When considering factors that influence academic progress and achievement in reading, environmental or external barriers to learning and performance cannot be minimized or discounted. Socio-cultural factors might involve socio-economic status, ethnic and racial identification, and culturally determined gender roles. These factors often play an integral role in the acquisition of reading skills necessary for academic success.

The number of students from diverse cultural and linguistic backgrounds has increased significantly in the United States over the past several decades. It is not uncommon for many of these children to arrive at schools with few or no English language skills. However, they bring into classrooms the cultural and linguistic values of their native countries. According to Heath (1986), schools must give equal consideration to the use of the English language and the particular languages students speak, as students' culturally acquired ways with words may be utilized to facilitate their learning of English literacy. Also, great care should be taken to avoid confusing cultural language barriers with learning disabilities.

Parents have an important role in this process. Some families are more attuned to school practices than others, and thus more inclined to engage in activities that enhance conventional literacy (Heath, 1983). It is important that educators understand the unique beliefs and practices that shape children's social and cultural environment. Parent and family relationships play an important role in the development of a child's self-esteem and capacity for coping with daily social and academic demands.

Students bring their problems at home to school. Domestic problems such as violence, alcoholism, drug use, unemployment, poverty, neglect, and mental illness frequently render children at risk for failure in reading and other academic spheres because of difficulty concentrating; controlling their behavior; and managing their anger, depression, and anxiety (Covington, 1989).

Wagner, Blackorby, and Hebbeler (1993) cite research to show that students with emotional issues fail more courses, earn lower grade point averages, have more days of absence from school, are retained in grade more than students with other disabilities, and are prone to dropping out of high school before graduation. Their vulnerability to failure is augmented by lack of academic and social supports, reactive teaching methods, and frequent displacement.

Educational Impoverishment and Progress

Reading failure may also be traced to inappropriate activities and methods used in schools (Humphrey, 1970). Progress in reading has a great deal to do with the classroom teacher's understanding of the child's readiness at any level and the methods by which learning occurs best. Progress is also contingent on efficient utilization of school resources and personnel that may be required. Skilled specialists and clinicians may sometimes be necessary, as specialized and individualized instruction may be required. However, this does not imply that reading or other disorders affecting academic achievement are the exclusive domain of special education. On the contrary, these problems must be addressed by the academic establishment and institutions at large.

The Individuals with Disabilities Education Act (IDEA; 2004) ensured that students with diverse learning disabilities, including reading disorders, receive specialized and individualized instruction to allow them the opportunity for a free and appropriate public education within the framework of a least restrictive environment. This landmark legislation passed on the heels of the 1975 Education for All Handicapped Children Act, which was designed to alleviate deplorable conditions of isolation and segregation for over 4.5 million children in the United States who had little or no access to quality public education because of their physical, mental, or emotional handicaps (National Council on Disability, 2000).

IDEA has profoundly changed the character of American education, allowing opportunity for remedial services to students who might otherwise be ignored and essentially disregarded in society. Although progress has been steady and impressive, there is still need for improvements. In many sectors, specialized services are provided separately from regular or mainstream education, creating conditions that promote homogenous groupings of children with learning disabilities, thus restricting the opportunity for mainstream providers to develop skills of diversified or differentiated instruction.

This is not to imply that individualized instruction provided within the framework of a contained setting may not be necessary, but self-contained special education instruction is still an overly used model. Within every school district, the emphasis needs to be on promoting a universal climate of ownership for all children, including those with disabilities and disorders.

A 2006 reauthorization of IDEA contains several significant elements related to literacy instruction, including early intervention, the use of a response to intervention model in providing services, and the implementation of evidence-based and research-proven strategies. This adaptation of IDEA authorizes schools to implement strategies for intervention and remediation before a child falls considerably behind grade level and before being eligible for special education services.

School districts are no longer bound to adhere to a "discrepancy model" to define a learning disability and can now find other ways to determine when a child needs extra help (Jimerson, Burns, & VanDerHeyden, 2007). In this regard, response to intervention encourages school wide "ownership" of students who are struggling with reading or other subjects and incorporates the opportunity for providing services to these learners who might otherwise be ignored.

REMEDIAL INTERVENTIONS

Reading Dysfluency

Interventions targeting specific mental functions that enable automatic recognition and recall of words have been successful in improving the reading process in children (Hale & Fiorello, 2004; Spafford & Grosser, 1996; Torgesen, Rashotte, & Alexander, 2001). Some of the most important principles recognized in reading fluency instruction include anticipatory facilitation, repetition, practice, and outside reading. Of those four general areas, the most effective method for increasing reading fluency is the application of repetition through repeated reading techniques (Myer & Felton, 1999).

Repeated reading involves both straightforward practice and simultaneous instruction and methods in which a student repeatedly reads letters, words, phrases, or passages a specific number of times or until a predetermined level of successful fluency is reached. According to a report by the National Reading Panel (2000), the repeated reading technique was found to be the only method that yields consistent and positive effectiveness in increased reading fluency.

Techniques involving repeated readings have similar effects as practicing the same song repeatedly on a musical instrument. As in music, repeated practice in reading can eventually lead to an improved level of automaticity or fluency. In a typical repeated reading exercise, a student can read a passage the first time through for accuracy, with an adult correcting initial mistakes.

Rereading the same passage will enhance automaticity and fluency. An additional strategy might involve keeping a chart of the time it takes to read the passages and the number of errors made, emphasizing both speed and accuracy. In addition, specific words a reader struggles with can be placed in a word bank, which can be reviewed at the beginning and end of each reading session.

Additional strategies for improving reading fluency skills include listening to an adult read, listening to books on tape while following along, and reading aloud with an adult (also known as "shadowing"). Many reading fluency remedial programs use and duplicate a combination of those processes and strategies, with the benefit of sophisticated and integrated aural and visual presentations that for most students also maintain high interest, often in "game like" formats.

Reading Disabilities

It has been shown repeatedly that remedial reading programs that specifically focus on instruction in phonological awareness and word decoding skills are more successful in improving the reading abilities of students who are weak in such skills when compared to interventions that do not emphasize phonological awareness (Wagner, Torgesen, & Rashotte, 1999; Wexler, Wanzek, & Vaughn, 2009).

Many established remedial reading programs focus on the development of phonological awareness and related phonics skills, and special education departments in most school systems will use standard structured reading programs when a student is determined to need help in phonological processing and phonics development. If a parent has questions or concerns regarding the structural remedial reading programs of instruction in phonological awareness and word decoding skills that a school system uses, the following points may be helpful:

* Reading decoding skills should be explicitly taught using a structured, developmentally progressive system. There are a wide range of such "linguistic" approaches to reading.
* Phonological analysis should be explicitly taught, demonstrating how words can be broken down into sounds. For instance, playing with rhymes and multisensory representations of sounds through visualizing and tapping out sounds can be utilized to promote phonological awareness.
* Students appear to learn better when decoding skills are taught using larger "chunks," such as word families, where patterns can be emphasized and fewer demands placed on memory.
* Reading decoding and word attack strategies first need to become automatic. "Guessing" at words should be discouraged.
* Spelling instruction should be taught in conjunction with the reading instruction program, using the same patterns or words utilized in reading.
* When a student with significant phonological processing delays is learning within the context of a remedial program, the highest success occurs when such instruction is offered by a qualified, experienced reading specialist; delivered on an individual basis or in a small group (two or three individuals); and conducted daily.

CONCLUSION

Reading disabilities, often referred to as dyslexia, represent a specific type of learning disability that involves a severe impairment in the reading process, which affects and disrupts a person's language development and functioning. The most common form of reading disability involves a deficiency in phonological processing capacities. Such deficiencies include problems with an early reader's phonological awareness capacities and related phonics skills.

Phonological processing refers to an individual's overall innate ability to hear, discriminate, recognize, and understand the various sound components in language. Phonological awareness, or the ability to hear and understand the sound-symbol correspondences of the printed page, is a critical component in the development of early reading skills.

A solid understanding of the various elements of phonological processing and awareness as well as the linguistic processes involved in literacy may provide parents and educators with a broader knowledge of the reading process and phonologically based reading problems. More familiarity with these reading-related processes can create a foundation for more informed use of field-specific terminology, enable the most effective assessment techniques, and suggest stronger remedial interventions for overcoming reading disabilities.

POINTS TO REMEMBER

- The basic characteristic of a reading disorder is an impaired ability to read. Relationships exist between reading disorders and expressive and receptive language.
- Three main processes are required for processing the written word: phonological processing, orthographic processing (processing speed), and comprehension.
- When assessing or developing an intervention for a reading disorder, it is critical to consider other factors that may hinder reading ability. To create a comprehensive reading intervention, the presence of attention deficit/ hyperactivity disorder or attention difficulties, sensory deficits, emotional and behavioral disorders, and socio-emotional issues will need to be considered and, if applicable, addressed.
- Remediation works best when programs focus primarily on phonological awareness and word decoding skills and target automatic mental processes.

REFERENCES

American Academy of Audiology. (2010). Clinical practice guidelines: Diagnosis, treatment, and management of children and adults with central auditory processing disorder. Reston, VA: Author.

Ashcraft, M. (1989). Human memory and cognition. Boston, MA: Scott, Foresman, and Co.

Badian, N. A. (1999). Reading disability defined as a discrepancy between listening and reading comprehension: A longitudinal study of stability, gender differences, and prevalence. Journal of Learning Disabilities, 32 (2), 138–48.

Barkley, R. (1997). ADHD and the nature of self-control. New York, NY: Guilford Press.

Birsch, J. R. (2005). Research and reading disability. In J. R. Birsch (Ed.), Multisensory teaching of basic language skills (p. 23–42). Baltimore, MD: Brookes.

Brady, S., Shankweiler, D., & Mann, V. (1983). Speech perception and memory coding in relation to reading ability. Journal of Experimental Child Psychology, 35, 345–67.

Cohen, G., Eysenck, M., & LeVoi, M. (1986). Memory: A cognitive approach. Philadelphia, PA: Open University Press.

Coleman, M., & Vaughn, S. (2000). Reading interventions for students with emotional/behavioral disorders. Behavioral Disorders, 25, 93–104.

Covington, M. (1989). Self-esteem and failure in school. In A. Mecca, N. Smeltzer, & J. Vasconcellos (Eds.), The social importance of self-esteem (p. 72–124). Berkeley, CA: University of California Press.

Crouch, E. M., & Dozier, P. M. (2011). Reading learning disorder. Medscape. Retrieved from http://emedicine.medscape.com/article/1835801-overview.

Daly, E., Chafouleas, S., & Skinner, C. (2005). Interventions for reading problems: Designing and evaluating effective strategies. New York, NY: Guilford Press.

Ghelani, K., Sidhu, R., Jain, U., & Tannock, R. (2004). Reading comprehension and reading-related abilities in adolescents with reading disabilities and attention-deficit/hyperactivity disorder. Dyslexia, 10, 364–84.

Glassberg, L. A., Hooper, S. R., & Mattison, R. E. (1999). Prevalence of learning disabilities at enrollment in special education students with behavioral disorders. Behavioral Disorders, 25, 9–21.

Hale, J., & Fiorello, C. (2004). School neuropsychology: A practitioner's handbook. New York, NY: Guilford Press.

Hallenbeck, B. A., Kauffman, J. M., & Lloyd, J. W. (1995). When, how, and why educational placement decisions are made: Two case studies. Journal of Emotional and Behavioral Disorders, 1, 109–17.

Heath, S. B. (1983). Ways with words: Language, life, and work in communities and classrooms. New York, NY: Cambridge University Press.

Heath, S. B. (1986). Socio-cultural contexts for language development. In Beyond language: Social and cultural factors in schooling language minority students (p. 143–86). Sacramento, CA: California State Department of Education, Sacramento, Bilingual Education Office.

Humphrey, J. M. (1970) Educational and environmental causes of reading problems. Paper presented at the third International Reading Association World Congress on Reading, Sydney, Australia.

Individuals with Disabilities Education Act. (2004) Retrieved from http://idea.ed.gov/explore/home.

Jimerson, S. R., Burns, M. K., & VanDerHeyden, A. M. (2007). Response to intervention at school: The science and practice of assessment and intervention. In S. R. Jimerson, M. K. Burns, & A. M. VanDerHeyden (Eds.), Handbook of response to intervention: The science and practice of assessment and intervention (p. 3–9). New York, NY: Springer.

Lange, S. M., & Thompson, B. (2006). Early identification and interventions for children at risk for learning disabilities. International Journal of Special Education, 21 (3), 108–19.

Logsdon, A. (2012). Learning disability in reading comprehension. About.com. Retrieved from http://learningdisabilities.about.com/od/learningdisabilitybasics/p/rdgcomprhnsn.htm.

Matlin, M. (1989). Cognition. Fort Worth, TX: Holt, Rinehart, and Winston.

Maughan, B., Pickles, A., Hagell, A., Rutter, M., & Yule, W. (1996). Reading problems and antisocial behavior: Developmental trends in comorbidity. Journal of Child Psychology and Psychiatry, 37, 405–18.

McCandliss, B. D., & Noble, K. G. (2003). The development of reading impairment: A cognitive neuroscience model. Mental Retardation Developmental Disabilities Research Reviews, 19 (3), 196–204.

Moats, L., & Tolman, C. (2009). Language essentials for teachers of reading and spelling (LETRS): The challenge of learning to read (Module 1). Boston, MA: Sopris West.

Myer, M. S., & Felton, R. H. (1999). Repeated reading to enhance fluency: Old approaches and new directions. Annals of Dyslexia, 49, 283–306.

National Center for Learning Disabilities. (1999). Visual and auditory processing disorders. Retrieved from http://www.ldonline.org/article/6390.

National Council on Disability. (2000). Retrieved from http://www.ncd.gov/.

National Reading Panel. (2000). Teaching children to read: An evidence-based assessment of the scientific research literature on reading and its implications for reading instruction. Washington, DC: National Institute of Child Health and Human Development.

Rayner, K., & Pollatsek, A. (1989). The psychology of reading. Upper Saddle River, NJ: Prentice-Hall.

Schank, R. (1982). Reading and understanding: Teaching from the perspective of artificial intelligence. Mahwah, NJ: Erlbaum.

Scheyer, M. G., Bishop, K. D., Jubala, K., & Coots, J. (1996). The inclusive classroom. Huntington Beach, CA: Teacher Created Materials.

Shaywitz, S. (2003). Overcoming dyslexia: A new and complete science-based program for reading problems at any level. New York, NY: Knopf.

Spafford, C., & Grosser, G. (1996). Dyslexia: Research and resource guide. Boston, MA: Allyn and Bacon.

Stanovich, K., & Siegel, L. (1994). The phenotypic performance profile of reading-disabled children: A regression-based test of the phonological-core variable-difference model. Journal of Educational Psychology, 86, 24–53.

Torgesen, J., Rashotte, C., & Alexander, A. (2001). Principles of fluency instruction in reading: Relationships with established empirical outcomes. In M. Wolf (Ed.), Dyslexia, fluency, and the brain (p. 333–56). Parkton, MD: York Press.

Valdois, S., Bosse, M. L., & Tainturier, M. J. (2004, November). The cognitive deficits responsible for developmental dyslexia: Review of evidence for a selective visual attentional disorder. Dyslexia, 10 (4), 339–63.

Vargo, F. E. (1992). Wechsler subtest profiles: Diagnostic usefulness with dyslexic children. Unpublished dissertation, American International College, Springfield, MA.

Vargo, F., Grosser, G., & Spafford, C. (1995). Digit Span and other WISC-R scores in the diagnosis of dyslexia in children. Perceptual and Motor Skills, 80, 219–29.

Wagner, M., Blackorby, J., and Hebbeler, K. (1993). Beyond the report card: The multiple dimensions of secondary school performance of students with disabilities. A report from the National Longitudinal Transition Study of Special Education Students. Menlo Park, CA: SRI International.

Wagner, R., Torgesen, J., & Rashotte, C. (1999). The comprehensive test of phonological processing: Examiner's manual. Austin, TX: Pro-Ed.

Wexler, J., Wanzek, J., & Vaughn, S. (2009). Preventing and remediating reading difficulties for elementary and secondary students. In G. Sederidis & T.A. Citro (Eds.), Strategies in reading for struggling learners (p. 28–53). Weston, MA: Learning Disabilities Worldwide.

Wiig, E., Zureich, P., & Chan, H. (2000, July/August). A clinical rationale for assessing rapid automatized naming in children with language disorders. Journal of Learning Disabilities, 33 (4), 359–74.

Wolf, M., Bowers, P. & Biddle, K. (2000). Naming-speed processes, timing, and reading: A conceptual review. Journal of Learning Disabilities 33, 387–407.

Chapter Six

Remedial Strategies Every Parent Should Know

Helping Struggling Middle School Readers

Julie DeRoach

Middle and secondary students are aware of their reading deficiencies, and parents carry the burden of this knowledge along with their children. Encouraging and supporting struggling readers must be an inclusive process between adolescent readers, families, and schools. McCray, Vaughn, and Neal (2001) cite Kos' (1991) research indicating that struggling readers "are cognizant of their deficiencies in reading" (p. 18). Armed with this knowledge and the resolve to support their children, parents have the unique ability to advance reading proficiency at home with their children.

IDENTIFY THE DIFFICULTY

Given that educators carve out time to teach intensive reading instruction in schools, parents have many options from which to choose when it comes to engaging their children in reading that motivates and supports literacy improvement at home. One of the first steps for parents to take is to "identify where the difficulty lies" ("Strategies to Help Engage Reluctant Readers in Reading," n.d., p. 1).

To begin, it is important for parents to recognize how a child acts when reading at home. Educators and parents should pay attention to the different types of texts middle school students are reading and the behavior these learners exhibit when reading various texts. As noted in "Strategies to Help

Engage Reluctant Readers in Reading" (n.d.), the following steps can help parents identify reading behaviors at home.

Over the course of several days, set aside time for reading and take notes about his or her reading behavior. Some of the questions you might want to ask yourself as you are observing your child are:

- How does your child react when you tell her it's time to read a book? Does she avoid reading? Is she nervous? Is she hesitant? Do behavior problems increase?
- What happens when your child begins reading? Does she have trouble staying focused on the text? Does she read slowly or too fast? Does she struggle to "sound out" or identify words? Does she misunderstand or not understand what she is reading?
- Does your child's attitude towards reading and ability to read a text change based on the reading material? Are certain topics more interesting to her than others? Are certain formats (i.e., books versus magazines) easier for her to read? (Strategies to Help Engage Reluctant Readers in Reading," n.d., p. 1)

With this information, parents can engage children in discussions about the types of books with which their adolescent readers are struggling. In addition, parents can better identify the types of intervention or attention that may be needed to support their struggling readers in the classroom.

MOTIVATING ADOLESCENT READERS

The development of positive and structured opportunities for struggling middle school readers at home entails the incorporation of many factors. The goal for families is to support their children with reading opportunities, helping them become more successful at reading. To do this, parents should continually promote reading-centered behaviors and activities and offer opportunities that engage adolescents in reading. When it comes to adolescent readers who are struggling with literacy, the ability to choose interesting texts is paramount.

Franzak's (2006) research highlights the many facets of adolescent reading and strategies that support adolescent reading in and out of school. Franzak (2006) cites Moje's (2000, 2002) assertion that the reading children do out of schools is not always viewed as purposeful reading or reading that is "valued in schools" (p. 221). Given that this is often the case, it is important for parents of struggling adolescent readers to engage their children where they are in their reading and to identify the preferences adolescents have when it comes to their reading. "School reading" and "engaged reading" may look different to parents and teachers, and it is essential for parents to guide their children towards reading that not only engages them but also supports their reading preferences.

CHARTING PROGRESS

Learning about the books that other children find worth reading is the next step in supporting struggling readers at home. When children are engaged in their reading, amazing things happen. Parents should begin to chart the information they are learning about their children and set goals to engage their children in collaborative reading opportunities. Setting goals for reading together with adolescents may sound more challenging than it really is.

To find out what adolescents are interested in, parents should visit websites and local bookstores to learn more about the types of books that interest adolescent readers. For example, every year, the American Library Association publishes an updated list of Newbery Award books. The Young Adult Library Services Association publishes the Top Ten for Best Fiction for these lists. In addition, grade-level and interest-based recommended reading lists exist on many town and school library websites.

In a recent study, Cavazos-Kottke (2006) took five gifted-and-talented readers to a bookstore to learn more about their personal reading preferences. This study was done to help teachers learn about readers', namely boys', attitudes towards choosing interesting reading material:

> [Boys in the study were] most interested in reading popular fiction (especially imaginary fiction, such as science fiction/fantasy novels), texts that have explicit connections to other media products, some literary classics, and both works of nonfiction that can be enjoyed aesthetically and works of fiction that can be enjoyed efferently. The author recommends providing opportunities for students to self-select personally interesting reading materials. (Cavazos-Kottke, 2006, p. 132)

Providing opportunities for children to self-select interesting reading material is critical to engage struggling adolescents in reading. Parents should make a conscious effort to take a monthly trip to the library or a local bookstore. This experience will become valuable for both parents and adolescents, and parents will be able to interact with their children in choosing suitable and engaging books. When adolescents have opportunities to identify books that interest them, parents will learn more about their reading preferences.

Choosing books, after spending time together in these locations, provides a chance for parents to select texts that they can read along with their children as well as texts that children can read independently. Perhaps families can make a list of other books that look interesting and plan to revisit the library or bookstore in upcoming weeks. When a child understands the expectation, it will add merit to building a literacy home front.

IDENTIFYING ROUTINES FOR READING

Locating a good book is easy compared to carving out the time that a child and parent will spend reading it together. But, rest assured, it can be done! As adolescents' lives tend to become busier during the school year, it may seem challenging to make specific time available for reading. Parents ought to come to consensus with their children regarding the establishment of a routine. When children learn the schedule and see that parents will follow through with it, they will come to expect that parents will engage in reading with them on a routine basis.

There are many strategies that parents can participate in when reading with their children, and parents also can set expectations for the children's independent reading. Here are some examples:

- Choose the number of chapters that will be read during the week.
- Keep an independent writing notebook or journal in which both parent and child can write any questions thought of during reading or note specific events and character traits that were interesting.
- Once a week, meet and discuss the focus of the journal writing. Make this fun by taking the child to a coffee house, a library, the park, or someplace interesting. Remember to make it meaningful and to stay on course.
- Parents can look for areas to take the children that will further the reading and learning. Are museums holding events that support the reading? Are there local activities, plays, social events, concerts, or movies that speak to the topic being read or that speak to the child's interests?

Building extension activities into children's reading makes reading the catalyst for engaging in aspects of life that expand on what children are learning. It is through these experiences that parents learn more about their children and can facilitate their learning in multiple layers. It is also in these experiences that families can notice what captures the interest of adolescent readers and through which they can build even more venues for reading. Remember that setting goals and following through with them while making reading fun is as important as picking out a book and bringing it home.

USING TECHNOLOGY TO SUPPORT READING

In twenty-first-century America, the vast majority of children are digital natives. In some cases, adolescents know more about technology than their parents do. Parents should learn about technology and the supports that technology can offer to struggling readers. Redford (2008) identifies the following examples for teachers and parents to support struggling readers via technology:

- Suggest listening to books on CD or identify a willing adult to read the assigned book to the student. Recommend that students read along with the CD version or follow the words alongside the reader. The more often a struggling reader is exposed to the way the words look, the better. Exposure to the page helps students learn the architecture of sentences. This also helps with spelling and conventions.
- Suggest use of assistive technologies currently available that read material aloud to the student. The Kindle would be an example of this kind of technology, but there are many similar devices being introduced into the market all the time.
- If the book/content has been made into a film or covered in a film, suggest that the student watch it to help give a context to the story or content. (p. 2)

In addition, parents can engage children with various reading supports: audiobooks, apps for reading, and blogs for readers. Educational apps for iPhones and iPads are constantly being created. Many apps, including Blio, Read2Go, and eTextbooks, allow parents to download stories that offer audio recordings of popular books, text-to-speech capabilities, and text highlighting. These resources will undoubtedly help struggling adolescent readers access material that is both popular and supportive to their reading needs.

RESEARCH-BASED STRATEGIES TO SUPPORT READING AT HOME

Word Study and Vocabulary

Implementing effective research-based strategies on word study, fluency, vocabulary, and comprehension to support struggling readers in the development of important skills will strengthen students' ability to read words more effectively. Parents can support children's vocabulary knowledge through activities that focus on the academic vocabulary words that students encounter in the content areas and through the introduction of new words.

As Boardman et al. (2008) state, "When students understand the meanings of the words they encounter in text and have strategies to figure out unknown words, they are more likely to understand the content of what they are reading" (p. 13). Struggling readers need repeated exposure to new strategies and must learn multiple meanings of words to access new content in school and to read increasingly difficult texts.

As a result of word study and vocabulary building, adolescent readers will gain an understanding of the words that will best support reading comprehension. Although the following word study practices are intended for classroom instruction, there is no reason why parents cannot use these strategies at home to help middle school readers:

- Teach students to identify and break words into syllable types.
- Teach students how to read multisyllabic words by blending the parts together.
- Teach students to recognize irregular words that do not follow predictable patterns.
- Teach students the meanings of common prefixes, suffixes, inflectional endings, and roots. Instruction should include ways in which words relate to one another (e.g., *trans–* in *transfer*, *translate*, *transform*, and *transition*).
- Teach students how to break words into word parts and to combine word parts to create words based on their roots, bases, or other features.
- Teach students how and when to use structural analysis to decode unknown words.

These strategies can be used by parents before or after shared reading. Teaching children how to recognize irregular words that do not follow patterns and how to identify prefixes, suffixes, endings, and roots can be done with word lists before or after reading. Lists of Latin and Greek root words as well as common prefixes and suffixes can be found at www.adlit.org.

Graphic Organizers for Vocabulary

Learning the meanings of new words can be accomplished through various strategies. One approach for supporting vocabulary learning is the early identification of challenging words. Other strategies include learning about words in both a visual and a conceptual format. If parents are reading books along with their struggling readers, reading ahead will allow for parents to identify words that may prove problematic for their children. After such words are identified, explicit, direct support and instruction on those words can be done through the use of graphic organizers.

Graphically studying words, their meanings, and the concepts that surround them will help students understand and visualize the relationships between words and their possible meanings. Often, students who struggle with reading need engaging strategies that help them visually organize new material, new words, and new ideas. One way to accomplish these different yet critical components of learning is through the use of graphic organizers.

Many websites for teachers include graphic organizer templates that can be easily copied or printed for use at home. At home, adolescents can do this work independently, and parents also should participate independently in this activity. A review and discussion of this material will aid vocabulary learning. For example, the Frayer model graphic organizer promotes critical thinking and allows students to identify words and concepts associated with a specific term or idea.

Another graphic organizer is a "concept map," which allows students to organize their thinking about specific concepts and make connections to specific topics related to each concept. The "List, Group, and Label" strategy also helps students identify words related to a topic and categorize words associated with each topic; this organizational strategy develops a better understanding of words and the concepts associated with certain topics.

These types of tools support struggling readers by helping students capture a deeper understanding of words. For a more in-depth list of strategies that can be used before, during, and after reading, visit the Adlit.org online strategy library to learn more about the different options available for home-based reading support.

Fluency

To support adolescents with reading fluency, researchers recommend that middle schoolers read selected passages from books or articles out loud with parent or tutor support. However, the following should be done before asking adolescents to read out loud at random:

- Select passages that students are interested in reading and that are appropriate for their independent or instructional reading level.
- Practice fluency with successive passages (in a novel or textbook) or a series of passages (short readings of similar difficulty). Do not have students reread the same passage repeatedly.
- As students' reading abilities improve, increase the complexity of the passage by selecting texts with challenging vocabulary and content.

Supporting opportunities for reading fluency is necessary to developing skills for adolescent readers. Research shows that "many adolescent struggling readers do not read fluently, even when they decode words accurately. . . . In addition to instruction in other essential areas of reading, students who read slowly and with difficulty should receive repeated opportunities to practice fluent reading orally with feedback from a more proficient reader—either a teacher or a peer" (Boardman et al., 2008, p. 9).

Comprehension

Supporting struggling readers' comprehension through varied strategy use is extremely important. McEwan (2007) advises teachers and parents to engage struggling readers in all of the following processes: activating, inferring, monitoring/clarifying, questioning, searching/selecting, summarizing, and visualizing/organizing. Figure 6.1 identifies and defines each of these comprehension-building characteristics.

Instructional Aid 1.1: Seven Strategies of Highly Effective Readers	
Strategy	Definition
Activating	"Priming the cognitive pump" in order to recall relevent prior knowledge and experiences from long-term memory in order to extract and construct meaning from text
Inferring	Bringing together what is spoken (written) in the text, what is unspoken (unwritten) in the text, and what is already known by the reader in order to extract and construct meaning from the text
Monitoring-Clarifying	Thinking about how and what one is reading, both during and after the act of reading, for purposes of determining if one is comprehending the text combined with the ability to clarify and fix up any mix-ups
Questioning	Engaging in learning dialogues with text (authors), peers, and teachers through self-questioning, question generation, and question answering
Searching-Selecting	Searching a variety of sources in order to select appropriate information to answer questions, define words and terms, clarify misunderstandings, solve problems, or gather information.
Summarizing	Restating the meaning of text in one's own words--different words from those used in the original text
Visualizing-Organizing	Constructing a mental image or graphic organizer for the purpose of extracting and constructing meaning from the text

Figure 6.1. Key Literacy Strategies for Middle Schoolers to Practice *Source:* **Copyright 2007 by Corwin Press, Inc. All rights reserved. Reprinted with permission from *40 Ways to Support Struggling Readers in Content Classrooms, Grades 6-12* by Elaine K. McEwan. Thousand Oaks, CA: Corwin Press, www.corwinpress.com**

According to Boardman et al. (2008), "Prior knowledge is the existing information students have about a topic, skill, or idea. Activating this knowledge helps students connect what they already know with what they are learning" (p. 23). Struggling readers may not automatically access prior knowledge that supports the new information they will learn, or they may access incorrect or unrelated information that can actually interfere with learning. Therefore, it is important to preview the text before reading to activate prior knowledge. Boardman et al. (2008) offer these suggestions:

- Use specific strategies to activate prior knowledge, such as previewing headings or key concepts, or making a prediction and confirmation chart.

- Prepare and guide previewing activities to support and focus the connections students make.
- Avoid soliciting guesses from students without guidance or feedback.
- Keep it short. Previewing should not take longer than five minutes.
- Revisit after reading to assist in reviewing, confirming or refuting predictions, summarizing, and making connections. (p. 23)

All these practices support comprehension and can be done in many different formats. Teaching adolescents how to activate their background knowledge and apply what they know about the topic or structure of the text supports the initial stages of text comprehension.

During reading, comprehension support can be achieved through various measures. In many cases, graphic organizers help students process and analyze information before, during, and after reading. Some strategies to use during reading include story maps, framed outlines, concept maps, and Venn diagrams (Boardman et al., 2008).

Research-based strategies include note-taking and summarizing strategies that support students' ability to retain information, check the information against the text, and make connections to the text. An extensive database of comprehension strategies, including organizing academic notes, cause-and-effect comparisons, comparison and contrast analysis, writing, Cornell double column notes, and much more, is available on the Greece [New York] Central School District's blue ribbon award-winning website (Deane-Williams, 2013).

CONCLUSION

Struggling readers have many opportunities to learn strategies for improving reading skills at home and at school. One of the most important characteristics to consider when organizing home-based support is to offer adolescent readers the ability to choose interesting texts. Allowing children to select engaging texts to work with sets the stage for investment in the process of reading and provides access to material from which adolescents can grow their reading skills.

All readers benefit from strategy instruction in the following components of reading: word study, vocabulary, fluency, and comprehension. There are an extraordinary number of opportunities, structures, and Internet resources available to children and families in support of home-based strategy instruction. Using rich and engaging literature, developing an understanding of adolescent reading, creating structure, and participating in supportive activities will develop stronger skills in struggling readers. As adolescents develop key literacy skills, they will build their own internal "reading strategy database," and they will learn to consistently apply the skills from this database to their future learning and academic achievement.

POINTS TO REMEMBER

- Parents can motivate the child to read at home by setting the example. They should set aside time each day to read together.
- Families ought to make regular trips to the library or bookstore. Opportunities to choose a book based on ability and interest should be paramount.
- Families who read together can keep a journal in which they discuss questions, define vocabulary words, and make predictions about what is to come in the book.
- Parents can look for outside activities that support reading and the child's interests.
- The use of assistive technology, such as an e-reader, online programs, text-to-voice features, or CDs can increase a child's understanding of the text.
- Reinforce word study and fluency skills through the use of graphic organizers.

REFERENCES

Boardman, A. G., Roberts, G., Vaughn, S., Wexler, J., Murray, C. S., & Kosanovich, M. (2008). Effective instruction for adolescent struggling readers: A practice brief. Portsmouth, NH: RMC Research Corporation, Center on Instruction.

Cavazos-Kottke, S. (2006). Five readers browsing: The reading interests of talented middle school boys. Gifted Child Quarterly, 50 (2), 132–47.

Deane-Williams, B. (2013). Tools for reading, writing and thinking. Greece Central School District. Retrieved from http://www.greececsd.org/academics.cfm?subpage=478.

Franzak, J. (2006). Zoom: A review of the literature on marginalized adolescent readers, literacy theory, and policy implications. Review of Educational Research, 76 (2), 209–48.

McCray, A., Vaughn, S., & Neal, L. (2001). Not all students learn to read by third grade: Middle school students speak out about their reading disabilities. Journal of Special Education, 35 (1), 17–30.

McEwan, E. K. (2007). Engage in teacher and student think-alouds daily. In 40 ways to support struggling readers in content classrooms, grades 6-12. (p. 7–13). Thousand Oaks, CA: Corwin Press.

Redford, K. (2008). Kids can't wait: Strategies to support struggling readers which don't require a PhD in neuropsychology. Retrieved from http://dyslexia.yale.edu/PRNT_EDU_KidsCantWiat.html.

Strategies to help engage reluctant readers in reading. (n.d.). K12Reader. Retrieved from http://www.k12reader.com/strategies-to-help-engage-reluctant-readers-in-reading/ .

Chapter Seven

Finding the Hook

Reeling in Reluctant Readers in the Middle Grades

Timothy C. Allen and Christine N. Michael

Engaging middle school students in reading is not an easy task. As students become young adolescents, their love of reading, which likely developed during the elementary years, often dissipates at the middle school level because of the conflicting interests of this age group. Friends, social media, sports, video games, and overall changing of preferred activities can move students away from reading as they become eleven, twelve, and thirteen years old. As eighth-grader Kristin says, "I don't read as much now as I did in elementary school because I am busier with homework and sports."

Another challenge that middle school teachers face as they attempt to promote continued literacy is that, in many ways, it simply becomes un-cool to enjoy reading. This perception is particularly powerful among preadolescent boys. Cam captures this sentiment by saying, "I am more into sports and just hanging out with my friends. I don't mean to be mean by saying this, but reading books is more for the nerdy boys."

Empathic middle school teachers know, too, that their students are caught up in a multitude of developmental tasks that absorb their energies. Kroger (2007) polled a class of early adolescents and found that the "Themes of changing biology pervaded their responses, followed by issues of wanting to fit in, to be normal, and to be liked by significant others" (p. 34). These salient issues were powerful enough to divert energies from almost all academic endeavors on a daily basis; however, there are approaches that can counterbalance these developmental draws.

Many teachers across the country find ways not only to keep middle school students interested in reading but to actually increase reading engagement during this developmental period. In this chapter, four award-winning teachers who have demonstrated success in encouraging middle school literacy share their strategies and highlight techniques that make middle school literacy a time of great excitement.

MARKETING

All four teachers agree that when it comes to middle school literacy, contemporary educators must function as salespeople in the classroom. Mr. Votto teaches eighth-grade English in a suburban middle school, having previously taught reading and English in an urban middle school. As Mr. Votto states, "In order to engage my students and to motivate them to read, there is only one phrase that really comes to mind: Sell it!"

Educators must create excitement around books and the act of reading. The days of passing out the classroom novel and implementing choral reading are truly over. To create middle school readers, the teacher plays a crucial role in igniting passion and interest. Books and topics must be introduced in ways that motivate students to become active participants.

Mrs. Brooks is a literacy coach in a suburban middle school, and she previously taught seventh-grade humanities in the Boston Public Schools. Without question, she views "marketing" as part of her role:

> We have to be marketers basically. Selling the books to the kids really works. I get a little excitement about something going; then I read a little bit to the kids. When they're ready, I have the kids start doing book talks. As the kids start recommending books, the excitement goes through your classroom like crazy. Part of class every day is having a book talk, whether it's me or a kid, and just talking about the book and why it was good. It's really the kids getting excited about things and getting other kids to want to read the same book.

Part of selling students on books and reading is to make the story come alive. Mr. Monroe, an assistant principal who has also been a literacy coach and a seventh-grade English teacher, employs strategies for making the book matter to students' lives:

> More than anything else, I believe it is important to make the learning come alive. You take what the students are reading and you make something from it so they can connect to it and sink their teeth into it. We did a number of cross-curricular units tied back to the text through field trips or project-based learning. You know, something that students can take away so that they remember the book and the life experience that went along with it. Anything we could do to engage the kids on that level helped reinforce the work.

In a similar vein, Mr. Monroe references work with his students during *The Hunger Games* phenomenon:

I thought it was incredibly important to jump on *The Hunger Games* when it was released, so I organized a One Book One School initiative outside of their English classes. To make the learning come alive, we made each classroom a different district from the book, had many activities, and then had a *Hunger Games* Field Day at the end of the book. This all stuck with the kids because the learning was coming alive.

Bringing in multimedia components also can help with the marketing of books. According to Mrs. Brooks, "Book trailers are great. And you can have students use technology to create their own book trailers. It is amazing how many kids want to read a book if you show a good book trailer." These uses of other media particularly benefit students whose primary learning style may not be visual or linguistic (Gardner, 2011).

Mr. Votto uses marketing after his students finish their books, too:

After we finished working with *The Giver*, I posted a list of books that had similar motifs, with the hopes of encouraging students to read more dystopian fiction. I also provided a list of novels that centered around the Holocaust when students finished *The Diary of Anne Frank*. In both cases, students seemed excited about delving further into these topics and themes on their own, despite our unit coming to an end.

PROMOTING PERSONAL INTERESTS AND CHOICE

Capitalizing on students' interests is another method teachers employ to improve middle school literacy. When students are introduced to books containing content that interests them or that they can personally relate to, they are far more likely to engage in reading. Mrs. Brooks discusses the importance of the personal connection to reading:

Finding out what kids' personal likes are and finding books that really talk to them is so important. I need to know something about their life, or their interests, or how they view the world. I do that with surveys or talking to the kids and getting to know them. One student I knew had a father in prison, and I hooked him through a book by Walter Dean Myers about a father who cuts out of prison and abducts his son, and they go across the country.

To secure the knowledge necessary to stock a classroom with interesting texts and make suggestions appropriate to each unique group of middle school readers, Murphy (2012) first conducts an interest survey with each student in her classroom; simple questions about habits, hobbies, and life aspirations populate her survey. After tallying the results of the survey, she uses a contemporary approach to turning the answers into reading materials for her students:

> Visit Google and set up various alerts using the answers you got on the survey. For example, if one of my answers was that a student wanted to be a marine biologist, I would set up an alert for marine biology, fish, sharks, and maybe underwater life.

She then prints out the articles and keeps topical binders for the students, matching each article with a predesigned question sheet that the student can complete after finishing the article. This approach to reading mimics the real-life reading that most of us do to research topics of personal utility and enjoyment. Her tactic also models how to be independent in finding answers to questions that students may have by conducting Internet research for an express purpose.

Mrs. Jackson, an eighth-grade English teacher in an urban school who is also a teaching coach and the English department chair, discusses at length the necessity of students having autonomy over their choice of books:

> Autonomy. They have to have choice regarding their reading material. I offer them a lot of different options. I always help them find the right book for the right reader. If there is a kid highly engaged in fantasy, they can find that in my classroom. If they are highly invested in realistic fiction, they can find that in my classroom. For the most part, it's just finding the right book for the right reader and just having a ton of materials in your classroom so that kids can make the best choice for themselves—and then guiding them in making those choices.

Wise teachers who recognize the need for autonomy in book choices validate a critical developmental task of early adolescence; according to researchers and theorists, the shift from dependence to independence is a primary job of the stage (Brown & Knowles, 2007; Caissy, 1994). As Brown and Knowles (2007) acknowledge, the effective middle school teacher will possess "a belief in the process of collaborating with students regarding curriculum and instruction" (p. 7). Mrs. Jackson astutely observes that narrow-mindedness among educators regarding book selections can be detrimental to students:

> A lot of teachers, especially English teachers, can be very judgmental about books. They don't feel like young adult books are like the classics. They don't have these multilayered plot lines. But we can't do that because we don't do that as adults. We pick books based on where we are in our lives. We pick books based on the experiences we are living right then and there. And students should do the same thing.

FINDING THE HOOK

Engaging middle school readers can be a multifaceted endeavor. Teachers must embrace the challenge and strategically work to encourage middle school literacy. Mr. Votto identifies an important part of this challenge:

> As far as engaging middle school readers, it is important to acknowledge that the majority of these students do not want to read in the first place. It is our job to select and implement challenging yet stimulating activities that leave them wanting more. I also think there sometimes is a disconnect, and some teachers just think that if they tell the kids to read the book that they will just do it. I find that holding them accountable by quick, little formative assessments here and there keeps them on their toes.

But Mrs. Brooks knows that "teaching them how to find just the right books is essential. Students get frustrated when they are reading books significantly above their reading level. It doesn't matter how engaging the content is if they can't understand what they're reading."

Interestingly, research demonstrates that struggling students can actually read more difficult materials if they are motivated to read them: "reading materials and teaching methods have a significant impact on students' motivation to read, regardless of students' reading ability" (Ivey & Broaddus, 2001). Finding inviting reading materials lies at the heart of quality classroom practice. Ivey and Broaddus' (2001) study identifies a theme that is repeated in other research: middle school students are highly motivated to read materials that are more reflective of the daily habits of adults (nonfiction, mysteries, reference books, series, and magazines) than the stuff of most language arts classrooms (textbooks and award-winning fiction).

Mr. Monroe also mentions the value of encouragement:

> So much of it was about just encouraging kids to want to read because once you open the door, the door is open for life. I was always under the firm belief that all it was going to take is finding the right book. Hook them! Hook them as best you can!

THE POWER OF RELEVANCE

Aside from choosing books that individual students can relate to, it is also possible to engage small groups or the whole class in reading when relevant and engaging topics are put forth. Sometimes, a student may not think a book will connect to him or her, but when the overall themes are introduced in an interesting manner, the book becomes surprisingly engaging.

Mr. Votto says,

> When I am about to teach a novel and the skills that accompany it, I strive to
> find relevant things to introduce the book and skills by pulling in some stimu-
> lating "prior knowledge" lessons. The goal of doing these lessons is to obvi-
> ously get the kids interested in reading but also to make them want to read it. I
> find that once students are excited about a topic . . . embedded within a
> text, . . . they simply just want more.

Mrs. Jackson concurs,

> The other thing I try to do is invest in books that have real-world situations—
> things that my students are encountering out in society. Maybe they are not
> directly encountering these experiences, but someone they know is, so I make
> sure they have those types of books in my classroom.

These teachers create classrooms that promote the kind of meaningful
learning that optimizes human development; they recognize that "all people
attempt to make meaning of the circumstances of their lives" (Brown &
Knowles, 2007, p. 154) and that during the middle school years, "a relevant
curriculum addresses issues that involve the cognitive, affective, and psycho-
motor domains while connecting to the lives and experiences of young adolescents" (Brighton, 2007, p. 17).

Connecting to the lives and experiences of today's adolescents with any
degree of authenticity involves the willingness to tackle subjects that many
might shy away from (see chapter 1). Mrs. Jackson asserts,

> I introduce books into the classroom that I don't think the typical English
> teacher would introduce. Books with heavy topics. I think about putting tough
> themes out there to kids, things that are happening in our society, and getting
> them to think about "Hey, can we change this?" And we learn from the experi-
> ence the character is going through. I think that invests kids.

Norton and Norton (2011) encourage the use of books on sensitive topics,
but they offer wise counsel to teachers as they make such book choices. The
following is among the advice they give: know what might be considered
controversial in one's school community, determine the author's point of
view and weigh the positive attributes of the book against the possible negative reaction, ascertain that the book is not chosen merely for high interest
because of its controversy but that it meets all standards for quality literature,
be able to explain articulately why the book was chosen, and be able to
discuss both sides of the censorship question intelligently.

When difficult but engaging topics exist within stories, teachers often
experience success introducing those topics before beginning the book. For
example, if a class is going to read *Where the Red Fern Grows*, the teacher

might start the unit by posing questions such as these: Why do kids fall in love with animals? How much would you work to buy the pet of your choice? How do you show your love for your pet? By involving students in these discussions, educators prepare their pupils for deep immersion in the story.

Mrs. Jackson describes this process in her classroom:

> I always lead with the topic, not the book. In every book, we have a theme. Even in nonfiction, there is a central idea. I always try to lead kids to think about themes that have to do with real life and then, I know that I'm looking for a certain theme or topic, but with students, just brainstorming a list of themes that can happen in a book or giving them a very brief summary and then thinking about what could happen in a book.

According to Mrs. Jackson, this prereading preparation may verge on the highly creative:

> With one eighth-grade class a couple of years ago, we did a novel titled *Staying Fat for Sarah Byrnes*. I introduced the book by presenting a picture of a burn victim that the kids had seen on the TV show *Dancing With the Stars*. He was a sergeant in the military, and he was severely burned, so I put a picture of him up at one of his worst points. We talked about as a class what might this person be feeling, what might this person go through in life looking this way. And from that list we came to a list of themes that might appear in *Sarah Byrnes* because she was a burn victim. Trying to think about the topics before we go into a book is always helpful. And then revisiting those topics doing things like theme tracking—writing about their own personal experience with a theme—helps us understand what's going on in a book.

"JUST READ"

Even when a teacher is able to practice all these strategies to increase reading engagement, students still must be afforded regular time designated for reading. With a seeming tsunami of mandated initiatives overtaking the classroom teacher, how does one find time to justify the "Drop Everything and Read" philosophy of quality literacy experts? Ivey and Broaddus' (2001) study on the motivating features of reading instruction highlight the importance of dedicated reading time. From a survey of 1,765 students across twenty-three schools, they discovered that students prefer silent reading time and teacher read-alouds more than any other reading activities.

Ivey and Broaddus (2001) also reported that students are motivated by having a choice in the materials that they read, citing that they read a far more diverse range of materials outside of school than in school. Students rue the lack of a wide variety of interesting materials in most of their classrooms.

If middle school teachers want to maximize the value of independent reading experiences, reading during these time periods must be valued solely for the pleasure that reading can bring, and it must embrace student choice about the reading materials.

After students select books that interest or excite them, they need time to read these books. As teachers noted, there is always a decision to make regarding class time. Can some time each day be saved for independent reading? Can the reading of independent books be incorporated in daily lessons? The teachers highlighted in this chapter are dedicated to providing independent reading time for students during the school day. Mrs. Jackson describes her belief in independent reading:

> I've always believed in autonomy over book choice, so we start with a lot of independent reading. That is another thing you have to let them do. My students become so upset when I don't give them time for independent reading. We have a ton of choice, a lot of materials, and the kids read. Using some of the strategies I teach in my mini-lesson, but not being forced. Just sitting down like we do as adults and just reading. Because of that, the kids devour large volumes of books.

In a results-driven environment, Mrs. Jackson has found the justification to link the pleasure of independent reading in the classroom with tangible, data-driven outcomes:

> You have to let kids just read. Every book that they come in contact with cannot be tied to a lesson. It can't be tied to annotating all the time, or putting sticky notes in it. Sometimes they just have to read. And they have to be given that time. If you give them that time, then by default you'll get better test takers. Because . . . to be a good test taker in a reading-and-writing situation, you have to be a good reader and a good writer. And the only way you become good at something is practicing. So they need time to *just read.*

INVOLVING THE FAMILY AND COMMUNITY

Even the best and most dedicated educators still grapple with how to engage families and the larger community in middle school literacy, as schools and teachers need involvement and reinforcement of literacy beyond their classroom walls. Families and communities are busy with many responsibilities and issues; connecting directly to middle school students is not often the top priority. However, when teachers are able to engage families or communities, the impact on student literacy can be profound.

Ferlazzo (2009) points out the critical difference between "involving" parents and actually "engaging" them in any initiative that the school undertakes:

When we're *engaging* parents, the parent is considered a leader or a potential leader who is integral to identifying a vision and goals. He/she encourages others to contribute their own vision to that big picture and helps perform the tasks that need to be achieved in order to reach those goals. When we're *engaging* parents, school staff act more as community organizers who help parents do things for themselves, and who elicit from parents ideas about what parents and school staff could be doing to better help their child and their community. (n.p.)

Meeting with parents and holding conversations about reading is a major step in Mrs. Brooks' classrooms: "I held a lot of conferences with parents and talked about the kind of books the kids would be interested in reading. I tried to educate parents that their kids are not necessarily going to read classic literature; it's really about getting them to keep reading what they love." Mr. Monroe agreed that the initial goal is communication: "It's harder to engage the families, but it is all about communication with families. As much as you can communicate, communicate!"

In many cases, families need to be reminded that they still play a key role in promoting their children's literacy; too often, family members assume that their adolescents' growing push for independence means that they no longer need be involved in reading with middle schoolers. As part of the communications process, teachers can share tips and websites that provide information pertinent to middle school literacy.

Scholastic (2015) touts several suggestions for families of adolescent readers. The first is to continue to read aloud with middle school students because they are not too old for this interaction; this interaction can take the form of alternating chapters with each other or suggesting that an older sibling read to a younger one. They offer other advice, such as modeling reading, keeping interesting reading materials in the home, setting limits on television and computer time to free up time for reading, talking about what family members are reading, and leaving time in preadolescents' busy schedules to just relax and read materials of their own choosing.

Moving beyond conversations and including families in actual literacy-centered activities is the next stage of engagement. Mrs. Jackson discusses methods for increasing families' participation in literacy:

> I taught in a sixth-grade class in an urban setting. At first, kids didn't read. When the parents noticed during the school year that they were reading more and more, we decided we needed to get students books at home. The kids just didn't have books of their own, so the parents and I did a book fair through Scholastic. It was very successful. All of the parents came out; they bought books for the kids. The books were discounted. And the parents supported it in an area where you don't often see a lot of parent support. The second one we did was at Barnes and Noble, and even though the parents didn't have transportation, they found a way to get out there and buy books for their kids.

Mr. Monroe stresses the importance of culminating activities that engage the larger community and describes one such initiative:

> We found some success while reading *Maus*, and the culminating activity was for students to go into the community and interview people at the local soldiers' home and the Jewish Community Center. Students took the information from the interviews and synthesized this with the themes from *Maus* . . . to create their own graphic novel. The student work was later displayed at the Basketball Hall of Fame, where students, families, and members of the community all came together. This community outreach event worked.

When students are engaging in reading, an indirect effect can be an increase in reading by other family members. Sometimes an adolescent gets excited about a book and takes it home; when the teacher asks the student where it is, the answer is that someone else at home is now reading it. If the student were really excited about reading it and then family members see him or her reading it voraciously, which is out of the norm for that child, it makes sense that they want to pick up the book also.

THE THRILL OF VICTORY

It certainly does not hurt to employ a little drama when stirring up interest in literacy activities. Swan Valley Middle School Principal Brad Erlenbeck did just that when kicking off his "Reading Month" initiatives. He entered the school gymnasium to start the Reading Challenge (reading one hundred thousand pages as a school during March) on a horse, wearing a Spartan costume, sword held high. "If you want to get kids excited, you've got to be a little zany yourself," he remarked.

In his first year as principal of Birchland Park Middle School in East Longmeadow, Massachusetts, Timothy Allen held a reading competition. Every book that a student read counted as a point, and at the end of the competition, the grade that read the most books duct-taped the principal to the wall in the cafeteria and fed him a hot pepper. Knowing there would be no water available for relief, the students were highly engaged in the competition. One parent even remarked casually that he had never seen his child read as much as he did for this competition.

Principals Erlenbeck and Allen are not alone in using friendly competition as a means to increase reading. Other schools report using external motivation in the quest to engage students such as organized programs with highly visible star power, such as the National Basketball Association's various Read to Achieve initiatives. The success of these efforts hinges on convincing young readers that powerful role models also value reading.

The New York Knicks, for example, promote reading via interactive videos and the Internet through the Read to Achieve program; successful readers earn team gear and tickets to games, while older students can participate in the Knicks Poetry Slam, which capitalizes on the popularity of hip-hop and poetry. The Boston Celtics reach out to empower blind children at forty-five local schools through collaboration with the National Braille Press. Some of these resources may be particularly helpful in reaching middle school boys who are reluctant readers.

CELEBRATING ACHIEVEMENTS

Encouragement also involves celebrating the successes of readers, especially those who are reluctant or struggling. The Southwest Educational Development Laboratory (2005) notes that "students who struggle with reading need consistent feedback on their efforts" (p. 15). The report further states that "the non-tangible incentives of teacher praise and constructive feedback have proven more motivational than the tangible rewards" (Southwest Educational Development Laboratory, 2005, p. 16), although tangible rewards, such as competitions and other activities, can spur reading as well.

Blow (2011) stresses that bribery rarely works as motivation but that positive reinforcement goes far because self-esteem is a need all students possess. As an example, she cites the "Got Caught Reading" wall outside sixth-grade teacher Dawn Sweredoski's room, where pictures of students who were caught reading Charlotte Award books are artfully displayed. Sweredoski, who is on the Charlotte Award Committee, receives hundreds of books annually from publishers to evaluate. However, she passes the books on to her students and gives them responsibility for reading, evaluating, and sharing their opinions. The students' feedback is posted on her wiki called *Read a good book lately?*

CONCLUSION

As a society, the level of public recognition of reading needs to be raised to the same level of recognition as sports, arts, and academic accomplishments. Because reading is critical both to academic and career success as well as the development of one's sense of self and inner life, marginalized readers need to be invited into the tradition of literacy and see their progress rewarded in a manner that reflects the value placed on other school activities.

Can teachers and students imagine a day when there is a readers' awards banquet equal to that of the annual sports awards celebration? By using the strategies suggested by researchers and the accomplished teachers featured throughout this chapter, schools, parents, and communities *can* recruit and engage reluctant middle school readers while keeping previously invested readers on the path of continued advancement throughout early adolescence.

POINTS TO REMEMBER

- Educators must work strategically to increase middle school students' engagement in literacy.
- Teachers must market books in the classroom to pique students' interest in reading.
- As often as possible, teachers should create situations in which students market books to one another.
- Matching students' personal interests with specific books will help hook students in reading.
- When teachers lead with interesting topics or themes, students will be more likely to engage in a text.
- Teachers must stock their classrooms with a wide range of interesting reading materials; families must do the same in their homes.
- Communication between education professionals and families regarding literacy and the creation of extended learning experiences also can improve middle school literacy.
- The achievements of middle school readers, especially those who are reluctant or struggling, must be celebrated.
- In addition to the above techniques, students also need time to *just read*.

REFERENCES

Blow, M. (2011, April 5). Motivating middle school students. Scholastic. Retrieved from http://www.scholastic.com/teachers/classroom-solutions/2011/04/motivating-middle-school-students?pImages=n&x=50&y=8.

Brighton, K. (2007). Coming of age: The education and development of young adolescents. Westerville, OH: National Middle School Association.

Brown, D. F., & Knowles, T. (2007). What every middle school teacher should know. Portsmouth, NH: Heinemann.

Caissy, G. A. (1994). Early adolescence. Cambridge, MA: Perseus.

Ferlazzo, L. (2009, May 19). Parent engagement or parent involvement? Learning First Alliance. Retrieved from http://www.learningfirst.org/LarryFerlazzoParentEngagement.

Gardner, H. E. (2011). Frames of mind: The theory of multiple intelligences. New York, NY: Basic Books.

Ivey, G., & Broaddus, K. (2001). "Just plain reading": A survey of what makes students want to read in middle school. Reading Research Quarterly, 36 (4), 350–77.

Kroger, J. (2007). Identity development: Adolescence through adulthood. Thousand Oaks, CA: Sage.

Murphy, D. (2012, May 17). Reading challenges. From Mrs. Murphy's Desk. Retrieved from http://motivatingmiddleschoolstudents.blogspot.com.

Norton, D. E., & Norton, S. (2011). Through the eyes of a child: An introduction to children's literature. Boston, MA: Pearson.

Scholastic. (2015). 17 ways to keep your middle schooler turning the pages. Retrieved from http://www.scholastic.com/parents/resources/article/more-reading-resources/17-ways-to-keep-your-middle-schooler-turning-pages.

Southwest Educational Development Laboratory. (2005, June). Reaching our reading goals. SEDL Letter. Retrieved from http://www.sedl.org/pubs/sedl-letter/v17n01/SEDLLetter_ v17n01.pdf

Chapter Eight

Popular Middle School Literacy and Intervention Programs

Research-Based and Teacher-Generated Approaches

Nicholas D. Young and Elizabeth Jean

Middle school students who have not yet mastered the fine art of reading and all its necessary components find themselves at a disadvantage when compared to their peers. If not quickly identified and remediated, this disadvantage can be "cumulative and profound" (Diamond, n.d., n.p.), potentially leading to high school dropout, the lack of entrance into college, and unemployment or the lack of adequate employment (Slavin, Cheung, Groff, & Lake, 2008).

As the expectations and rigor of research projects, testing, class work, and even homework grows, students must be able to comprehend and attach meaning to words. Students with reading difficulties may try to hide their disability and frustrations, thus leading to greater problems within the classroom (Diamond, n.d.). For these reasons, it is imperative to help students remediate reading struggles quickly and efficiently.

Equally important is the need to ensure that teachers are adequately trained to use research-based programs. Pure implementation is not enough and may fail for the following six reasons:

1. Insufficient training to teach the program
2. Lack of coaching throughout the year to support program implementation
3. Program-specific requirements (both groupings and scheduling) that lack fidelity in implementation
4. Implementation lacked sufficient intensity to close the learning gap

5. Lack of progress monitoring by teachers
6. A plethora of initiatives distilled the implementation, support, time, and resources (McPeak & Smith, 2011)

Quality research-based reading programs designed specifically to meet the unique learning gaps of middle school students are vital. These programs must "take into account a lack of background knowledge, delayed language development, and limited successful reading experiences" (Diamond, n.d., n.p.). Many programs claim to be research based, yet they lack the substance necessary to live up to that designation.

For middle school students to overcome their learning gaps, three critically necessary components are required to design, implement, and sustain any reading interventions: effective professional development, instructional tools aligned with schema, and systemic reorganization and support (Diamond, n.d.).

Professional development is necessary to ensure fidelity in using a research-based intervention program (Slavin, Cheung, Groff, & Lake, 2008). A one-and-done approach will not support educators in training or understanding the intervention and how it best serves student needs. Ongoing professional development, however, provides sustained learning on the part of the educator and allows for a trial-and-error period in which to learn through modeling, practice, and feedback. Another important piece of professional development would include coaching, which increases the fidelity of implementation by as much as 90 percent (Diamond, n.d.).

Instructional tools are necessary components of any reading intervention meant to close the middle school reading gaps and include the motivation to read, decoding skills, fluency, language comprehension, and text comprehension. Each of these instructional tools plays a critical role in student success; however, interventions that disregard decoding and fluency miss the primary skill deficit in middle school students (Shaywitz et al., 1999).

In terms of systemic leadership and support, the school administration must commit to implementation with fidelity of any research-based intervention program. The administration is responsible for professional development, scheduling, and resources. In addition, the administration must take into consideration the need for regular assessment, both formative and summative. Not to be left out of the overall intervention picture is the necessity of the home-school connection. Students need to know that their families value and support the learning by engaging in home reading programs as well.

This chapter will now describe and explain some of the research-based interventions and programs used by middle school educators to increase reading ability. Programs vary widely, and research-based programs are few and far between for the middle school child. For this reason, some instructional practices that will aid students in reading remediation have also been included in this chapter.

ONLINE-DIRECTED INTERVENTIONS AND PROGRAMS

Accelerated Reader (AR) is an online supplemental intervention program produced by Renaissance Learning. This system first assesses each individual student's reading level with an online test called a STAR reading test (Renaissance Learning, 2013). As the student reads the multiple-choice test questions and answers them correctly, the test becomes more difficult. If the student misses an answer, the test complexity is reduced. The test process takes about fifteen minutes, and once complete, a printable list of suggested reading materials based on the correct student reading level is produced.

Students read books in their selected range and then take an online quiz to prove their reading comprehension of that particular text. Each book is given a difficulty level, and students are awarded a certain number of points based on correct answers. Students must answer more than 60 percent of the questions correctly to pass the quiz and move on to another text. Librarians and teachers use the online software to "keep detailed records of what books students read and whether they pass the computer-scored quiz" (Chenoweth, 2001, p. 51).

According to Renaissance Learning (2013), there are five different types of quizzes in the AR program that "support the development of several reading skills" (p. 5):

1. Reading practice quizzes that determine comprehension and offer immediate feedback. These are the most common assessment used in AR.
2. Recorded voice quizzes that are used by beginning readers and those students who are just learning English. These quizzes utilize a professional narrator.
3. Vocabulary practice quizzes that are meant to increase word recognition and acquisition using authentic text.
4. Literacy skills quizzes that are based on "[twenty-four] specific, higher-order reading comprehension skills" (Renaissance Learning, 2013, p. 5). These skills are taken from standardized tests, a variety of state standards, and basal readers.
5. Other reading quizzes that are aligned to particular textbooks to test student comprehension of specific material.

With over 156,000 titles, AR includes texts that run from kindergarten through grade twelve, making the program accessible to readers of all levels.

Whether the child is gifted or struggling, AR offers a challenge to students and a chance for struggling readers to find success in reading, increasing self-esteem and pushing the reader to want to read more often. In addition, parents are able to go online and access student progress information, thus offering support in finding interesting books to read as well as enthusiasm surrounding the reading process.

Other online intervention systems, such as Josten's Compass Learning (Compass Learning, 2014), similarly use a set of assessments to determine where to begin student learning within their educational continuum. Students work individually while completing their online activities, which are meant to address their personal learning gaps. The program is accessed by students two to five days a week, and each activity typically takes between fifteen and twenty minutes to complete.

Both AR and Compass Learning are strictly online, and as such, there is no professional development necessary for teachers. Both systems are meant to be used in conjunction with other interventions to provide a wide continuum of educational experiences specifically meant to increase student success and self-esteem in all aspects of reading and comprehension skills.

TEACHER-DIRECTED INTERVENTIONS AND PROGRAMS

Making Connections Intervention

Making Connections Intervention (MCI) is a blended learning system developed by Kay Kovalevs and Allison Dewsbury that combines online and print-based work for targeted literacy intervention for struggling readers at the middle school level (Balajthy, 2014). MCI is interactive and systematic in nature, as students begin online with a pretest and assessment tests to gauge students' initial level of learning and then return for post-testing after a particular gap has been mastered. This type of monitoring allows teachers to see precisely where individual student gaps are and how to remediate them.

MCI features several curriculum parts, including comprehension, writing, word study, and technology. Each curriculum is entwined with the others and empowers students through choices that provide struggling readers with a much-needed dose of self-esteem. MCI provides such options at the end of each unit in summative activities, including individual book choice and cooperative learning (Balajthy, 2014).

Making Connections Intervention's Literacy Curriculum: Comprehension

The National Reading Panel and the Common Core State Standards identify eight key factors needed to improve comprehension in struggling readers (Balajthy, 2014), and each of these factors are used by the MCI program:

1. Comprehension monitoring: This component involves making sure students recognize how they gain meaning from text. Self-monitoring and correcting one's self is a taught skill that will increase reading ability by making students aware when things do not make sense.
2. Cooperative or collaborative learning: Students work in pairs or small groups on learning tasks. Students rely on one another for corrections and increased discourse, which will increase comprehension by its very nature (Slavin, Cheung, Groff, & Lake, 2008).
3. Graphic organizers: Visual representation of prior knowledge (and new knowledge) helps the reader organize information for better comprehension.
4. Text structure: Preteaching text structure ensures that students have a basic understanding of patterns used in narrative stories, allowing them to retain meaning by concentrating on structural elements that in turn improve their ability to recall events in the story (Scharer, Lehman, & Peters, 2001).
5. Question answering: Answering teacher- and student-generated questions is a proven method to improve recall. Teachers use this approach as a way to understand what the student has retained.
6. Question generation: Student-generated questioning allows students to gain a clearer idea of what they want to find out while reading the story as well as to better understand parts of the story that may have been confusing when discussing a text after the initial reading.
7. Summarization: Using summarization helps students remember the text by pointing out major ideas and important details within the story.
8. Multiple strategies: As with any learning, students and teachers must use a wide range of strategies to increase learning and comprehension when interacting with text (National Reading Panel, 2000).

Making Connections Intervention's Literacy Curriculum: Writing

Writing is a necessary part of the reading process. Many state-mandated tests (Partnership for Assessment of Readiness for College and Careers, for example) and the Common Core of State Standards assess composition as a skill that students must be able to exhibit as young as second grade. The MCI writing curriculum is based on four traits (Balajthy, 2014):

1. Reading-writing connection: Using various literary genres and text structures to increase student interest in writing improves both composition and comprehension. When taught explicitly and to mastery, students are better able to emulate these structures in their own writing (Graham & Perin, 2007).

2. Writing skills and strategies: The use of formal writing strategies (planning, revising, and editing) elevates the level of student writing, according to Graham and Perin (2007).
3. Writing in the content areas: Common Core underscores the importance of writing within the content areas across the grade levels as a way to increase student understanding of the content areas.
4. The writing process: Regardless of the writing curriculum used (Lucy Calkins, Traits 6+1, Donald Graves, etc.), the process—with teacher support to increase the depth of knowledge—remains the same: composing, planning, drafting, revising, editing, and publishing.

Making Connections Intervention's Literacy Curriculum: Word Study

Students may have trouble with pronunciation, deriving meaning from a word, or both. Whether decoding or vocabulary is the issue, MCI uses two facets within the literacy curriculum to guide and remediate struggling readers.

1. Phonics and structural analysis: Students who cannot decode words easily generally have poor fluency skills because of the amount of time they must spend sounding out words or skipping over them. Word recognition leads to fluency, which will increase comprehension. Equally important is morphology (structural analysis) in which students need to be able to make meaning from root words, prefixes, and suffixes.
2. Vocabulary: Students' word banks grow as they learn to make meaning from "words used to describe their world" (Balajthy, 2014, n.p.). Consequently, educators should use new words within the context of something the students already know, repeat them often to ingrain the words, and have students intimately involved in the process (Nagy & Scott, 2000).

Making Connections Intervention's Use of Technology

Undeniably, the digital natives of today use technology to gain knowledge of all kinds (Prensky, 2010). They are often more comfortable in front of technology than a teacher. They are able to find information quickly and use technology easily. Using a rotation model of part-teacher/part-technology, MCI recognizes these realities and sees them as opportunities to increase participation and understanding among struggling middle school students:

• Blended learning, e-learning, and new literacies: These learning modalities use a combination of online and brick-and-mortar learning to expand the student knowledge base using neuroscience concepts (Greenfield, 2011).

- Effectiveness of computer-based, online learning: According to the National Reading Panel (2000), online learning was found to have positive results, and a blended learning situation was found to be more effective than sole online learning. Thus, to improve reading comprehension and vocabulary achievement in digital natives, blended learning would appear to be optimal.
- Audio and visual technology: "Audio technology allows students to listen to words and repeat as needed for clear pronunciations, while video is a multisensory way to present information" (Balajthy, 2014, p. 14).

Clearly, MCI has covered all the bases by using a response to intervention model that includes assessment and reporting. The program engages struggling students in many different ways and uses research-based methods to increase their overall comprehension, fluency, and word study. Using the Common Core State Standards as a guide, MCI coordinates lessons and finds texts at various levels to challenge all readers.

Voyager Passport

Voyager Passport boasts an intensive program for below-grade-level students. There is a whole-group component as well as partner practice and flexible, small-group instruction. A technology component includes DVDs, activities, and instruction strategy practice surrounding vocabulary, fluency, comprehension, and writing.

READ 180

Currently marketed by Scholastic, READ 180 was originally developed in 2004 by Hasselbring and Goin at Vanderbilt University. READ 180 features reading intervention for students who read between a grade level of 1.5 to 8. Instructional periods are ninety minutes long, and each group can consist of up to fifteen students. Students begin with a twenty-minute shared reading session as well as a skill-based mini-lesson (Slavin, Cheung, Groff, & Lake, 2008). Students then rotate between three stations: (1) guided reading with the teacher, (2) modeled or independent reading, and (3) computer-assisted instructional reading.

Educators receive professional development, including materials and workshops. The workshops target reading strategies, word study, vocabulary, and comprehension. Students use the technology component to read about science and social studies topics and complete activities that include word study, vocabulary, comprehension, fluency, and strategies used by strong readers (Slavin, Cheung, Groff, & Lake, 2008). There are also leveled paperback books for students to read, covering a wide gamut of genres and ensuring all students can find a topic of interest.

Orton-Gillingham

Orton-Gillingham is named after its creators, Samuel T. Orton (1879–1948), a physician and neurologist, and Anna Gillingham (1878–1963), a teacher and psychologist, both of whom were interested in working on reading difficulties. Orton found that multisensory instruction integrated both sides of the brain, making the learning easier. Gillingham, using the work completed by Orton, produced and published manuals for systematically teaching the forty-four phonemes as well as other decoding strategies, giving students rules to follow (Reading Horizons, 2014).

Initially used for the remediation of dyslexia, these same principles can also be applied to help middle school students with reading struggles. The Orton-Gillingham program consists of lessons in various formats, including whole group, small group, and individual. It focuses on phonemic awareness, phonics, fluency, vocabulary, and comprehension. According to the National Reading Panel (2000), evidence shows that "explicit, systemic phonics instruction is a valuable and essential part of a successful classroom reading program" (p. 222).

According to the International Dyslexia Association (2000a), Orton-Gillingham instruction is multifaceted and includes the following five main principles of instruction:

1. Multisensory teaching: Kinesthetic, auditory, and visual cues activate memory and written language.
2. Systematic and cumulative structures: Alphabetic and phonemic principles are learned sequentially and with a cumulative effect. Scaffolding allows students to accumulate knowledge in an organized fashion.
3. Direct instruction: Instruction is delivered in a variety of teacher-student formats.
4. Continuous educator assessment: Planning is based solely on the data obtained from student assessment to inform instruction.
5. Synthetic and analytic instruction: Using synthetic (parts to whole) and analytic (whole to parts) instruction allows students to grasp a concept and internalize it for future use.

Perhaps the most important aspect of the Orton-Gillingham approach is the utilization of multisensory teaching. Consistently allowing students to make connections between what they see (visual), hear (auditory), and feel (kinesthetic) provides a "conscious organization and retention of their learning" (International Dyslexia Association, 2000b, n.p.). This learning is the scaffolding that then helps struggling students make progress in a plethora of reading skills and in overall comprehension.

Comparable systems, such as the Sonday System, developed by Arlene Sonday, were created based on the Orton-Gillingham method. The difference, however, is that the Sonday System is less cumbersome to learn, requiring no special training other than a ninety-minute video that acts as a how-to for teachers and parents. Detailed lesson plans are included along with multisensory activities and techniques. The Sonday System provides a scaffolding of learned skills that allows students to progress and retain all necessary information.

Literacy Collaborative

Known as the Literacy Collaborative, this research-based reading model is the work of Irene Fountas and Gay Su Pinnell. It is grounded in a two-pronged, multiyear approach that includes professional development and instruction models. Within each model, specific traits and training opportunities allow schools to improve their teaching and learning in the areas of reading, writing, language, and word study as they connect to Common Core State Standards and response to intervention (Literacy Collaborative, 2014).

The Literacy Collaborative's Professional Development Model.

The professional development model begins with identifying and training a literacy coach as well as building a school-based leadership team. The team may consist of administrators, teachers, the literacy coach, and any other person who is involved with reading and writing. During year one, the literacy coach is involved in rigorous training, while the team is tasked with developing goals and outcomes, building a home-school connection, and creating a plan for measuring student progress (Literacy Collaborative, 2014).

Year two begins with professional development, classroom implementation, and coaching support; these continue to be the foci for the next three years. Professional development for educators includes becoming proficient with the language and literacy framework as well as understanding the rationale and theory that influence the Literacy Collaborative. Educators must be able to implement the program with fidelity, refine their skills, and learn how to monitor student progress to move learners forward.

Year five is dedicated to continued whole-school professional development and specific educator coaching. The main focus, however, is to become proficient at analyzing data and evaluating student growth as a means to refine and enhance not only student learning but effective teaching (Literacy Collaborative, 2014). The Literacy Collaborative takes this one step further, using the data, parent/student surveys, observations, and interviews as a way to guide and improve the learning process.

The Literacy Collaborative's Instructional Model.

The foundation for the instructional model begins with Fountas and Pinnell's (2009) *The Continuum of Literacy Learning*, which describes "specific behaviors and understandings expected in the areas of reading, writing, language, and word study" (Literacy Collaborative, 2014, n.p.). This book resembles the Common Core State Standards, and coaches and educators are expected to use both documents to inform instruction.

No less important is the Literacy Collaborative's language and literacy framework. This framework provides student-centered learning opportunities focused on word study, oral language development, and phonics. Authentic reading and writing opportunities abound using workshop models in both areas. Educators are able to differentiate instruction using whole-group, small-group, and individual instruction as well as balance individual student-inquiry learning with teacher-directed experiences (Literacy Collaborative, 2014).

Followed precisely, research showed significant literacy learning growth with students involved in the program versus the baseline group (Biancarosa, Bryk, & Dexter, 2010). Results were impressive, with a jump from 16 percent versus the baseline in year one to 32 percent at the end of year three (Biancarosa, Bryk, & Dexter, 2010). These gains were evident despite the usual summer slide. This same research suggested that the gain resulted primarily from the coaching expertise (through the professional development model) and its direct effect on teaching.

INSTRUCTIONAL PRACTICES FOR MIDDLE SCHOOL READING PROGRAMS

While there are a limited number of research-based middle school reading programs and interventions that appear to have lasting effects on student outcomes, tried-and-true instructional practices can often make the difference for struggling students. The following are examples of practices, strategies, and techniques meant to increase decoding, phonemic awareness, phonics, vocabulary, comprehension, and fluency. As noted, they are collected from numerous sources, including educators, research studies, and educational journal articles:

• Cooperative learning in small groups: Students help one another to understand and master specific skills. The success of the group is dependent on each member's participation (Slavin, 1995).

- Modeling strategies: Regardless of the strategy (decoding, prior knowledge, preview and predicting, inferencing, etc.), it is important for the teacher to repeatedly model it so that students understand what it looks and sounds like.
- Guided practice with gradual release: Guided practice occurs in small groups or an individual basis. The teacher leads students in reading text with the expectation that they will be able to then go read independently.
- Independent practice: Reading independently for fluency and comprehension is the next step after guided reading.
- Rituals and routines: An example would be "Ask Three Before Me," in which a student would look for peer support prior to going to the teacher.
- Accountable talk: Used as a way to provide rich feedback and reduce anxiety in students, accountable talk uses key phrases for all students in a positive manner (e.g., "I agree with Sally because . . . " or "I disagree with John because . . .").
- Read authentic texts for real-world reasons, such as research.
- Large amounts of time ought to be spent reading. Here, quantity is as important as quality.
- Classrooms should contain a diversity of genres to read.
- Vocabulary and concept development flourishes in environments where words and their meanings are regularly discussed and understood.
- Time spent writing texts creates an understanding of how text and writing weave together (Duke & Pearson, 2002).
- Meaningful, high-quality discussions about texts should include student-to-student and student-to-teacher conversations.
- Making text-to-text, text-to-self, and text-to-others connections is a valuable way to increase schema and scaffold understanding.
- Reading out loud to create fluent readers: Fluency practice should contain challenging text. Four best practices are (1) echo reading, as it provides the most scaffolding for struggling readers; (2) choral reading; (3) partner reading; or (4) reading and listening to text simultaneously (Meisinger & Bradley, 2008).
- Flashcard drill and practice: After teacher modeling has occurred, repeated showings of the card for mastery by the child have been proven to help mostly with unknown words (Joseph, 2008).
- Graphic organizers: When students have been shown how to use story maps or webs, these visual comprehension guides facilitate the comprehension of key themes and details as well as walking through the entire story (Joseph, 2008).

CONCLUSION

Middle school students find the most difficulty in decoding and fluency, with a close second being text and language comprehension. As the academic workload increases in complexity, adolescent students become more frustrated. To address the needs of middle school students who face such frustrations, administrators and teachers must be cognizant of the literacy intervention program chosen and use it with fidelity. Adequate professional development and the ability to work with the research-based program outside of student time is a must if it is to be used correctly. Above all, a connection must be made with the families of these struggling middle school readers. Although building a home–school connection is not an easy task, families and students who work together find the most success in conquering reading difficulties.

POINTS TO REMEMBER

- Because the primary reading deficit of middle school students involves decoding and fluency, all literacy and intervention programs must address these skills.
- Instructional tools, whether purchased or teacher-generated, should motivate students to read and address not only fluency and decoding but boost text and language comprehension as well.
- The school administration ought to take an active role in implementation and consider all forms of assessment to increase skills.
- Professional development is vital to implementation with fidelity, as educators need to be given ample time to understand the program.
- The home–school connection cannot be ignored; connections among teachers, students, and parents will build bridges that improve learning.

REFERENCES

Balajthy, E. (2014). MCI (Making connections intervention). Retrieved from https://eps. schoolspecialty.com/EPS/media/Site-Resources/Downloads/research-papers/series/MCI_ research.pdf?ext=.pdf.

Biancarosa, G., Bryk, A. S., & Dexter, E. R. (2010). Assessing the value-added effects of literacy collaborative professional development on student learning. Elementary School Journal, 111 (1), 7–34.

Chenoweth, K. (2001). Keeping score. School Library Journal, 47(9), 48–51.

Compass Learning. (2014). Guided by research. Propelled by fun. Retrieved from http://www. compasslearning.com.

Diamond, L. (n.d.). Implementing and sustaining a middle and high school reading and intervention program. Oakland, CA: CORE. Retrieved from https://www.corelearn.com/files/ CORE-SecondaryReading.pdf.

Duke, N. K., & Pearson, P. D. (2002). Effective practices for developing reading comprehension. In C. A. Stone, E. R. Silliman, B. J. Ehren, & K. Apel (Eds.), What research has to say about reading instruction (3rd ed., p. 205–42). Newark, DE: International Reading Press.

Fountas, I. C., & Pinnell, G. S. (2009). The continuum of literacy learning. Portsmouth, NH: Heinemann.

Graham, S., & Perin, D. (2007). Writing next: Effective strategies to improve writing of adolescents in middle and high schools. Washington, DC: Alliance for Excellent Education.

Greenfield, S. (2011). The quest for meaning in the 21st century. London, England: Hodder and Stoughton.

International Dyslexia Association. (2000a). Just the facts: Orton-Gillingham based and/or multi-sensory structured language approaches. Retrieved from http://www.dys-add.com/resources/Myths/IDA.OG.Fact.Sheet.pdf.

International Dyslexia Association. (2000b). Multisensory teaching. Retrieved from http://www.bartonreading.com/pdf/IDA-SimultaneouslyMultisensory.pdf.

Joseph, L. M. (2008). Best practices on interventions for students with reading problems. In Best Practices in School Psychology (Vol. 4, p. 1163–80). Retrieved from https://www.killeenisd.org/teacherDocs/c53/e2914/documents/ReadingLiteracy-85368.pdf.

Literacy Collaborative. (2014). Literacy collaborative. Retrieved from http://www.literacycollaborative.org/index.php.

McPeak, L., & Smith, F. A. (2001, May). A systematic approach to the implementation of research-proven interventions for struggling readers gr. 4-12. Paper presented at Sonoma County Office of Education, Sonoma, CA.

Meisinger, B. B., & Bradley, B. A. (2008). Classroom practices for supporting fluency development. In M. R. Kuhn & P. J. Schwanenflugel (Eds.), Fluency in the classroom (p. 1–5). New York, NY: Guilford Press.

Nagy, W. E., & Scott, J. A. (2000). Vocabulary processes. In M. Kamil, P. B. Mosenthal, P. D. Peterson, & R. Barr (Eds.), Handbook of reading research. Vol. 3. (p. 269–84). New York, NY: Erlbaum.

National Reading Panel. (2000). Teaching children to read: An evidence-based assessment of the scientific research literature on reading and its implications for reading instruction. Washington, DC: National Institute of Child Health and Human Development. Retrieved from http://www.nichd.nih.gov/publications/pubs/nrp/documents/report.pdf.

Prensky, M. (2010). Teaching digital natives: Partnering for real learning. Thousand Oaks, CA: Corwin.

Reading Horizons. (2014). Orton-Gillingham method. Retrieved from http://athome.readinghorizons.com/solutions/orton-gillingham-2.

Renaissance Learning. (2013). Parent's guide to Accelerated Reader. Retrieved from http://doc.renlearn.com/KMNet/R003985016GG79F2.pdf.

Scherer, P. L., Lehman, B. A., & Peters, D. (2001). Pondering the significance of big and little or saving the whales: Discussions of narrative and expository text in fourth and fifth-grade classrooms. *Reading Research and Instruction*, 40(4), 297-314.

Shaywitz, S. E., Fletcher, J. M., Holahan, J. M., Shneider, A. E., Marchione, K. E., Stuebing, K. K., et al. (1999). Persistence of dyslexia: The Connecticut longitudinal study at adolescence. Pediatrics, 104 (6), 1351–59.

Slavin, R. E. (1995). Cooperative learning: Theory, research, and practice. 2nd ed., rev. Boston, MA: Allyn and Bacon.

Slavin, R. E., Cheung, A., Groff, C., & Lake, C. (2008). Effective reading programs for middle and high schools: A best-evidence synthesis. Reading Research Quarterly, 43 (3), 290–322.

Chapter Nine

Applying the Response to Intervention Framework to Reading Challenges

A Multifaceted Approach

Jennifer S. Alexander and Nicholas D. Young

As secondary schools seek solutions to ensuring that students are both college and career ready for twenty-first-century learning, there is a sense of
urgency to provide instructional support services to students who are reading
below grade level compared to their peers. The competitive nature of the
global economy as well as decreased demands for factory workers and farm-
ers, give rise to students who are leaving high school academically unpre-
pared to face the employment challenges of the twenty-first century.

In addition, students who are retained or consistently performing below
grade level are at risk for dropping out of school. "Children who are not
reading at grade level by age nine are ten times more likely to drop out of
school before receiving a high school diploma" (Buffum, Mattos, & Webber,
2009, p. 62). Addressing the demands and needs of high-risk students is an
ongoing challenge faced not only at the local level but at the national level as
well. At-risk students are generally minority youth who are economically
disadvantaged.

If gaps are not filled to provide a successful climate and setting for at-risk
students, the potential for the students to drop out is astounding. According
to *Silent Epidemic: Perspectives of High School Dropouts*, "There is a high
school dropout epidemic in America. Each year, almost one third of all
public high school students—and nearly one half of all blacks, Hispanics,
and Native Americans—fail to graduate from public high school with their
class" (Milliken, 2007, p. xxi).

This high rate of dropout students places a financial hardship on the country because of the increasing welfare, social service, and medical needs of unemployed high school dropouts. "*Each youth* who drops out of school and later moves into a life of crime or drugs is costing the nation somewhere between \$1.7 and \$2.3 million" (Milliken, 2007, p. xxii–xxiii). It would be far more beneficial for society to be proactive and implement strategies that focus on dropout prevention.

There is also a correlation between high school dropout and crime: "Someone who didn't graduate is more than eight times as likely to be in jail or prison as a person with at least a high school diploma. Half of all prison inmates are dropouts. In fact, on any given day, more young male dropouts are in prison than at a job" (Milliken, 2007, p. xxii).

The consequence of not finding ways to prevent students from dropping out of high school is devastating to the individual and the nation. Addressing learning gaps early on in the student's education fosters future academic growth and readiness. Students who are well equipped and demonstrate academic proficiency are less likely to drop out.

In 1983, the National Commission on Excellence in Education's *A Nation at Risk* examined the educational system and highlighted the tragic effects of an ill-prepared society caused by the inadequacies of teacher readiness, instruction, funding, resources, technology, and global competitiveness: "Each generation of Americans has outstripped its parents in education, in literacy and in economic attainment. For the first time in the history of our country, the educational skills of one generation will not surpass, will not equal, will not even approach, those of their parents" (p. 6).

In 2008, the U.S. Department of Education published *A Nation Accountable*, and though some improvements were noted in the areas of curriculum content, teacher quality, and instruction, students are still falling behind and continuing to drop out of school: "Educational quality directly affects individual earnings, and dropouts are much more likely than their peers who graduate to be unemployed, living in poverty, receiving public relief, in prison, on death row, unhealthy, or single parents" (p. 11).

Based on research, studies, and data, high school dropout rates are a significant concern among policymakers, state agencies, private industry, community members, and parents. When students drop out of school, their ability to find a decent-paying job is greatly diminished in comparison to their peers who complete high school. Investing time, effort, and resources while students are still in the school system is a necessary reality that school leaders must address to provide meaningful solutions.

RESPONSE TO INTERVENTION

Response to intervention (RTI) provides academic and behavioral supports for students who are performing below grade level. RTI is designed to meet the needs of all types of students: English language learners, general education, special education, talented and gifted, and struggling. RTI also creates open lines of communication between the schools and families in developing effective strategies towards student achievement.

Within the intervention model, there are three tiers of instruction with differing levels of intensity to address the academic and behavioral needs of students. The premise of RTI is to identify the learning outcomes of students and develop specific interventions that address concerns about student achievement and engagement.

In this model, teachers, guidance counselors, psychologists, literacy coaches, speech-language pathologists, reading specialists, and administrators come together to ask critical and meaningful questions about student learning. Questions may include:

- Why didn't the student meet the targeted goal?
- What can be done differently to help students reach proficiency?
- What systems and supports need to be in place to help struggling students?
- How will student progress be monitored?
- What changes need to be made in the daily schedule to create opportunities for interventions?

Designed to meet the individual needs of a student, RTI helps the learner make gains academically and behaviorally. The National Center on Response to Intervention (n.d.) offers the following definition for RTI:

> Rigorous implementation of RTI includes a combination of high quality, culturally and linguistically responsive instruction; assessment; and evidence based intervention. Comprehensive RTI implementation will contribute to more meaningful identification of learning and behavioral problems, improve instructional quality, provide all students with the best opportunities to succeed in school, and assist with the identification of learning disabilities and other disabilities. (n.p.)

RTI offers a systematic and comprehensive approach to address varying levels of student progress. The National Center on Response to Intervention website (www.rti4success.org) provides essential information, scheduling templates, and tools for successful RTI implementation.

Response to Intervention Components

The National Center on Response to Intervention maintains that there are four essential components of RTI:

1. Universal screening
2. Progress monitoring
3. A multilevel prevention system
4. Data-based decision making

A universal screener is a criterion- or norm-referenced assessment. A norm-referenced test can be administered one to two times a year, generally at the start and the end of the school year. Teachers and administrators use this data to gauge student growth throughout the school year. Schools also administer benchmark assessments during the school year to assess student growth and progress suitable to a student's grade level and content-area learning goals. Cut points from the assessments are used to place students in appropriate tiers of instruction.

Student support teams or data teams also refer to state exams in addition to school benchmarks and norm-referenced assessments when determining student interventions. Teacher input and feedback on student behavior, work habits, and performance on class projects and assignments offer a general overview of the student's progress within the classroom setting.

Progress monitoring is essential in determining how students are growing and developing with the interventions. In a middle school setting, grade-level or student support teams meet on a consistent basis to review student progress. The school schedule should allocate time for teacher collaboration. During the meetings, members discuss and share student progress. If students are not making continued progress with the interventions, the student may need more intensive support and will move from Tier 2 to Tier 3 support.

A multilevel prevention system consists of three tiers of instruction:

*   Tier 1 provides a core curriculum for all students.
*   Tier 2 offers small-group instruction that targets specific learning needs for students through evidence-based interventions with moderate intensity.
*   Tier 3 consists of individualized, intensive, and frequent interventions.

Students within all tiers of instruction have access to Tier 1, a core curriculum of instruction and support. The course of study and materials are typically determined at the school or district level. In a middle school setting, student proficiency in reading comprehension can be assessed through a comprehension assessment such as a Scholastic Reading Inventory.

The Scholastic Reading Inventory provides a student lexile level; teachers can use this lexile score to identify the students' independent and instructional reading levels. This information assists in selecting appropriate reading materials to supplement core reading texts for social studies, science, and independent reading. Administrators and teachers can identify students for intervention services based on data reports generated from the inventory. Parents receive information pertaining to their child's lexile score, recommended reading material, and strategies to support their child's reading.

In addition to providing a research-based core program, schools must identify "essential" or "power" standards. Teachers work collaboratively to analyze and identify standards that are necessary for student mastery and readiness for the next grade level. Buffum, Mattos, and Webber (2009) state, "A school that has significantly less than 75% of its students at or above grade-level has a core program problem, not an intervention problem" (p. 74). Implementation of a research-based core program with effective instruction and identified essential standards is imperative for student learning.

Students receiving Tier 2 support participate in small-group instruction lasting ten to fifteen weeks of twenty- to forty-minute sessions three or four times a week beyond core instruction. During this time period, the teacher or specialist will continue to monitor progress to inform and guide instruction. The staff uses research-based programs designed to provide appropriate interventions to improve the students' reading skills.

Tier 3 instruction is more intensive with smaller groups as well as longer and more frequent sessions. The teacher or specialist conducts weekly progress monitoring to determine the rate of student improvement and to identify specific areas of academic concern. After those areas are identified, the teacher will design and provide strategic and intensive intervention through research-based programs.

Differentiated Instruction

It is necessary that classroom teachers are able to interpret ongoing assessment data from both formative and summative assessments to differentiate instruction within the classroom setting. Buffum, Mattos, and Webber (2009) help explain the need for differentiated instruction by explaining that "The most important step a school can take to improve its core program is differentiating instruction and small-group activities" (p. 74). This effective form of instruction allows the teacher to identify specific strengths and weaknesses and design instruction in a meaningful, engaging manner to ensure student development and understanding.

Heacox (2002) provides more detail stating, "Differentiated instruction means changing the pace, level, or kind of instruction you provide in response to the individual learner's needs, styles, or interests" (p. 5). Tomlinson and Moon (2013) further define differentiated instruction as consisting of five components: content, process, product, affect, and the learning environment. All these elements are differentiated to address students' readiness, interests, learning profiles, or preferences.

Students who demonstrate mastery can engage in independent activities, projects, or computer software programs that can challenge student learning. Students are also provided the choice to select specific learning activities that complement their talents and interests. Those students who need additional instructional support can work in a small-group setting with the classroom teacher, while others are working independently on material appropriate to their academic needs and interests. The differentiated classroom provides flexible grouping and appropriately designed tasks.

To facilitate both small groups and independent lessons, it is important that educators can manage a classroom effectively. "Teachers play various roles in a typical classroom, but surely one of the most important is that of classroom manager. Effective teaching and learning cannot take place in a poorly managed classroom" (Marzano, 2003, p. 1). A classroom that functions efficiently with minimal interruptions will find that more time is spent on learning, and meaningful conversations between students take place.

When students are actively engaged in learning activities that foster and promote a sharing of ideas, they are learning valuable concepts from one another. The teacher plays a key role in creating this community of learners. Established routines and procedures are imperative for an organized and well-managed classroom. Students must know the expectations for their behaviors, actions, and responsibilities.

Intervention Programs and Instructional Practices

Effective use and implementation of an RTI model alleviates the misdiagnoses of students with learning disabilities. Through interventions and consistent progress monitoring, students receive necessary academic support, thereby potentially reducing the number of students referred for special education services.

Data-based decision making is necessary to RTI implementation. Data from universal screening, benchmarks, formative and summative assessments, and state-level assessments provide essential information when determining appropriate interventions for students. Establishing cut points allows the data team to identify intervention for tiered instruction. However, cut points alone are not sufficient. To meet the needs of students, teachers, specialists, and instructional leaders must have the latitude to problem solve. Engaging in candid conversations about student performance and concerns is vital to supporting and assisting students.

Within a professional learning community, schools provide interventions that are appropriate to the types of learners. There are two types of learners: the intentional non-learner and the intentional learner. "Intentional non-learners are neither motivated by grades nor aware of the long-term implications for failing in school. They simply resist doing what they don't want to do" (Buffum, Mattos, & Webber, 2009, p. 89). The intentional learner tries to learn the material through effort, yet the student does not make the expected academic gains.

"In contrast, to intentional non-learners, failed learners have attempted to learn but have yet to demonstrate proficiency. The problem is not that they won't do the work, but that they don't know how" (Buffum, Mattos, & Webber, 2009, p. 91). To meet the needs of the intentional non-learner, schools may provide extra help sessions, extended day programs in the morning or after school, study skills classes, goal setting or incentive programs, and frequent communication with parents.

Interventions provide appropriate and targeted services that support the academic needs of struggling students. The U.S. Department of Education's Institute of Education Sciences What Works Clearing House (www.ies.ed. gov/ncee/wwc) provides research on programs, products, practices, and policies related to education. The website offers information on educational resources and interventions for educators to make evidence-based decisions. The following are some intervention programs and instructional practices taken from the What Works Clearing House:

- **Accelerated Reader** is a guided reading intervention used to supplement regular reading. The program is designed to improve students' reading comprehension through practice reading and quizzes.
- **Class Wide Peer Tutoring** is an instructional strategy to integrate with reading curriculum. Students are provided with opportunities to practice reading, ask questions, and receive feedback from peers based on taught strategies.
- **Cooperative Integrated Reading and Composition** is a reading and writing program that consists of three elements: story-related activities, direct instruction in reading comprehension, and integrated language arts/ writing.
- **Corrective Reading** is a program designed to develop decoding, fluency, and comprehension skills.
- **FastForward** is a computer-based program designed to help students develop and improve cognitive skills for reading and learning.
- **Peer Assisted Learning Strategies** consists of students working in pairs to read aloud, listen to the partner read aloud, and provide feedback during structured reading activities to improve reading fluency and comprehension.

- **Project Creating Independence through Student-owned Strategies** is a professional development program for teachers that derives from cognitive psychology and brain research and that aims to improve reading, writing, and learning for students.
- **READ 180 Next Generation** is a comprehensive and systematic intervention program designed to improve reading skills. Its components include whole- and small-group instruction, independent reading, and adaptive instructional software targeted to meet the needs of individual learners.
- **Read Naturally** incorporates a strategy of teacher modeling, repeated reading, and progress monitoring to improve reading proficiency, accuracy, and fluency. The reading program includes books, audiotapes, and computer software.
- **Reading Apprenticeship** is an instructional approach to help students develop skills and knowledge to improve engagement, fluency, and comprehension of content-area materials and texts.
- **Reciprocal Teaching** is an instructional strategy that allows the student to fill the role as the teacher and facilitate a small-group discussion in the areas of summarizing, question generating, clarifying, and predicting to improve reading comprehension.
- **SpellRead** is a small-group literacy program that integrates the auditory and visual aspects of the reading process and emphasizes specific skill mastery through systematic and explicit instruction.
- **Student Team Reading and Writing** is an integrated approach to reading and language arts through cooperative learning, a literature anthology, and explicit instruction. The reading program includes cooperative classroom processes, high-interest reading, and explicit reading comprehension instruction. The writing component includes learning teams, teacher presentation, practice, peer preassessment, and individual assessment.
- **Success for All and Reading Edge** are schoolwide comprehensive programs that include interventions, leadership, instruction, and professional development. The model includes a reading, writing, and oral language development program.
- **SuccessMaker** is an adaptive instructional software program that provides students with instructional support in phonological awareness, phonics, fluency, vocabulary, comprehension, and concepts of print.

RESPONSE TO INTERVENTION IMPLEMENTATION

To facilitate RTI implementation of a tiered approach to instruction and intervention, strong leadership and a supportive school structure are crucial. Establishing a cohesive partnership between teachers, support staff, administrators, and families is inherent to the success of RTI. Professional learning communities can create a school culture that fosters and promotes collaboration and opportunities to problem solve. In establishing such a community, there are three "big ideas" to consider (DuFour, DuFour, Eaker, & Karhanek, 2010).

The first big idea guides the work of schools and districts: "The fundamental purpose of the school is to ensure that all students *learn* rather than to see to it that all students are *taught*—an enormous distinction" (DuFour, DuFour, Eaker, & Karhanek, 2010, p. 7). The second big idea is that a professional learning community requires a collaborative and supportive culture to account for student learning and answering critical questions surrounding student achievement. The third big idea is the use of assessments and data to determine appropriate instruction and interventions for students. Teachers and administrators share assessment results and make collaborative decisions in the best interests of the students.

To meet the needs of the students, schools must allocate time for daily intervention, academic support, and enrichment. This structure may require schools to reconfigure the master schedule to include a period for interventions. This flexible type of schedule allows teachers to recommend students for interventions, and groups of students can receive interventions based on assessment data.

School Leadership

Sustainable leadership understands the nature of student learning and engagement. "The origins and underpinnings of the idea of sustainability really matter; they give it its moral substance, conceptual precision, and strategic power" (Hargreaves & Fink, 2005, p. 21). The quality of the students' education is at the forefront of the school's leadership team. Instructional practices are frequently discussed, and teachers are encouraged to develop and refine teaching practices. With learning as the focal point of the school's vision, high-stakes tests are not emphasized. Rather, administrators and teachers discuss student learning, analyze data, and collaborate on an ongoing basis.

With RTI, student achievement is a long-term goal instead of a "quick-fix" approach. A sustainable methodology emphasizes learning, achievement, and then testing. Deep and broad knowledge prepares students for the challenges and experiences they will face in life. Learning that is rigorous and relevant engages the student emotionally, mentally, and physically. Strong faculty and learner relationships allow teachers to understand their students and customize the educational process for the individual needs of each student.

Effective leaders empower staff members. A principal must utilize the expertise and knowledge of colleagues to develop a strong and cohesive school. Distributive leadership allows for a shared and collaborative approach to decision making and problem solving. Teachers, parents, and administrators can contribute their ideas and opinions to facilitate change within an institution. Empowering staff members to take on leadership roles provides venues for teacher development, personal growth, and teamwork.

When teachers are involved in the transformation process, the longevity and endurance of the initiated efforts are more likely to last. Student achievement improves as teachers become part of the systematic change process by sharing instructional strategies, offering professional development, and conducting peer observations.

Moral Commitment

As schools focus on preparing students to think critically and become productive, conscientious citizens, school leaders must be mindful of the behavior and environment that is cultivated within the school community. What beliefs are perpetuated? What does the school stand for? How do the routines, principles, and activities impact the culture of the school? School leaders and teachers have a moral commitment to create an environment that perpetuates a system of change to improve student learning. Within morality stands the purpose and reasoning behind policies, decisions, and procedures to improve a school:

> If school leaders do not take their moral imperative on the road, system transformation will be impossible because you can't change the system from the center or from weakly supported grassroots networks. The new moral imperative implicates all school leaders in a shared mission to improve all schools. (Fullan, 2003, p. 59)

The leadership within a school building plays an important role in the future development of students and the impact those students will have on society.

Parental Involvement

Parental involvement is integral to the success of a student's academic performance. Parents can reinforce taught strategies and increase time on learning while at home. When parents become part of the learning process and embrace this role to assist their child, the student will receive additional support within the home environment. Inviting parents to meetings will help promote a strong relationship between the school and the family.

Through time, effort, and hard work, this team approach will lead to the academic and behavioral progression of the student. Harmon and Dickens (2007) explain: "Successful teachers and schools implement practices that enable schools to support families and families to support schools" (p. 14).

Continued communication efforts between parents and educators help to put students' needs at the forefront.

Consequently, parents are incapable of assisting if the teacher's concerns are not communicated. Whether the concerns are about academics or behavior, parents can implement strategies recommended by the teachers or support staff to provide consistency between the school and the home. Both educators and parents can support methods of reinforcement to meet the needs of middle school adolescents; this collaborative approach lets students know that there are consequences and expectations for both the classroom and the home setting.

CONCLUSION

RTI is a support system that provides academic and behavior interventions within a three-tier model. RTI meets the needs of a variety of students and creates a home–school connection that improves academic and behavioral success. The four components of RTI (i.e., assess, monitor, intervention, and data-based decisions) allow students to flow between the tiers in a quest for intervention success. RTI provides differentiated instruction through personalized programs and instructional practices. When supported by school leadership and families and used with fidelity, RTI helps students succeed with the joint support of teachers and parents.

POINTS TO REMEMBER

- If gaps are not filled to provide a successful climate and setting for at-risk students, the potential for students to drop out is astonishing.
- RTI is designed to provide academic and behavior supports for students who are performing below grade level and have not reached proficiency, and it is intended to meet the needs of English language learners as well as general education, special education, talented and gifted, and struggling students.
- RTI offers a systematic and comprehensive approach to address varying levels of student progress.
- School leaders play an integral role in the development and implementation of a tiered support system to meet the academic and behavioral needs of students.
- Parents can support children through strong, effective communication between the home and school.

REFERENCES

Buffum, A., Mattos, M., & Webber, C. (2009). Pyramid response to intervention, professional learning communities, and how to respond when kids don't learn. Bloomington, IN: Solution Tree.

DuFour, R., DuFour, R., Eaker, R., & Karhanek, G. (2010). Raising the bar and closing the gap: Whatever it takes. Bloomington, IN: Solution Tree.

Fullan, M. (2003). The moral imperative of school leadership. Thousand Oaks, CA: Corwin Press.

Hargreaves, A., & Fink, D. (2005). Sustainable leadership. San Francisco, CA: Jossey-Bass.

Harmon, H., & Dickens, B. (2007). Creating parent and family involvement. Timberville, VA: Professional Consulting and Research Services.

Heacox, D. (2002). Differentiating instruction in the regular classroom. Minneapolis, MN: Free Spirit.

Marzano, R. (2003). Classroom management that works: Research-based strategies for every teacher. Alexandria, VA: Association for Supervision and Curriculum Development.

Milliken, B. (2007). The last dropout: Stop the epidemic! Carlsbad, CA: Hay House.

National Center on Response to Intervention. (n.d.). What is RTI? The essential components of RTI. Retrieved from http://www.rti4success.org/essential-components-rti.

National Commission on Excellence in Education. (1983). A nation at risk: The imperative for educational reform. Retrieved from http://datacenter.spps.org/uploads/sotw_a_nation_at_risk_1983.pdf.

Tomlinson, C., & Moon, T. (2013). Assessment and student success in a differentiated classroom. Alexandria, VA: Association for Supervision and Curriculum Development.

U.S. Department of Education. (2008). A nation accountable: Twenty-five years after A Nation at Risk. Washington, DC: Author. Retrieved from http://www2.ed.gov/rschstat/research/pubs/accountable/accountable.pdf.

About the Primary Authors

NICHOLAS D. YOUNG, PHD, EDD

Dr. Nicholas D. Young has worked in diverse educational roles for more than twenty-five years, serving as a principal, special education director, graduate professor, college dean, and longtime superintendent of schools. He is a former Massachusetts Superintendent of the Year, and he completed a distinguished Fulbright program focused on the Japanese educational system through the collegiate level. Dr. Young holds numerous degrees, including a PhD in educational administration and an EdD in educational psychology. He has served in the U.S. Army and U.S. Army Reserves combined for over thirty years and is a graduate of the U.S. Air War College and the U.S. Army War College, and is currently a student in the U.S. Naval War College. Dr. Young is a Colonel in the U.S. Army Reserves and recently completed his tenure as the commander of the 399th Combat Support Hospital in Devens, Massachusetts, before transitioning to a faculty position at the U.S. Army War College. Dr. Young is a regular presenter at state, national, and international conferences, and he has coauthored or authored many books, book chapters, and articles on various topics in education, counseling, and psychology. His most recent work includes coauthoring *Collapsing Educational Boundaries from Preschool to PhD: Building Bridges Across the Educational Spectrum* (2013) and *Learning Style Perspectives: Impact Upon the Classroom* (3rd ed., 2014), as well as being a primary author/co-editor of *Educational Entrepreneurship: Promoting Public-Private Partnerships for the 21st Century* (2015), *Betwixt and Between: Understanding and Meeting the Social and Emotional Developmental Needs of Students During the Middle School Transition Years* (2014), and *Transforming Special Education*

Practices: A Primer for School Administrators and Policy Makers (2012). Dr. Young may be contacted at nyoung1191@aol.com.

CHRISTINE N. MICHAEL, PHD

Dr. Christine N. Michael is a thirty-year educational veteran with a variety of professional experiences. She holds degrees from Brown University, Rhode Island College, Union Institute and University, and the University of Connecticut, where she earned a PhD in education, human development, and family relations. Her previous work has included middle and high school teaching, higher education administration, college teaching, and educational consulting. She has also been involved with Head Start, Upward Bound, and the federal Trio programs and has published widely on topics in education and psychology. Her recent work included serving as a primary author and co-editor on the book *Betwixt and Between: Understanding and Meeting the Social and Emotional Development Needs of Students During the Middle School Transition Years* (2014). Dr. Michael may be contacted at cnevadam@gmail.com.

About the Chapter Authors

JENNIFER S. ALEXANDER, EDD

Dr. Jennifer S. Alexander serves as the administrator of student interventions and McKinney-Vento homeless liaison for the Westfield Public School District in Massachusetts. In addition, she is a member of the Committee of Practitioners for the Massachusetts Department of Elementary and Secondary Education Title I Office and a member of the Council of Administrators of Compensatory Education. She has held many teaching and administrative roles during her career in public education. In 2006, she was the recipient of the Grinspoon Pioneer Valley Excellence in Teaching Award. She is a regular presenter and has published on family and school partnerships and the application of response to intervention to social and emotional challenges. She earned a BA in English from the University of Washington as well as an MEd in elementary education, a CAGS in school administration, and an EdD in leadership and supervision from American International College. She can be contacted at alexander6771@gmail.com.

TIMOTHY C. ALLEN, EDD

Dr. Timothy C. Allen is currently the principal of Birchland Park Middle School in East Longmeadow, Massachusetts. Prior to assuming this position, he was principal of an urban middle school in Springfield, Massachusetts, as well as assistant principal of two urban middle schools. He also has served as a middle school English teacher, an elementary teacher in the Bronx, and an English instructor in a juvenile detention center. He earned an EdD from American International College, a CAGS from the University of Massachusetts, an MA from Columbia University Teachers College, and a BA from Wheaton College. Dr. Allen is an adjunct professor at American International College and Our Lady of the Elms College. He can be contacted at tca19782@gmail.com.

JULIE DEROACH, EDD

Dr. Julie DeRoche holds a BA in English from Northeastern University, an MS in Reading and Literacy from Wheelock College, and a CAGS and EdD in Educational Leadership from American International College. As an educator with twenty years' experience, she has served in a variety of positions during her career in education, including English teacher, college professor, and educational consultant. Julie has presented in state and national educational conferences on topics in reading, literacy, and science, technology, engineering, and mathematics, and is published in *Powerful Partners in Student Success: Schools, Families and Communities* (2012). Julie is a full-time Director of Curriculum and Instruction for a public school system in Massachusetts. She may be contacted at derochej@georgetown.k12.ma.us.

SANDRA DONAH, EDD

Dr. Sandra Donah has worked in the field of special education for the past twenty-four years, mainly as a special education teacher at all levels. She is currently a director of special education in Massachusetts. She is also the clinical director of Western Massachusetts Learning Centers for Children, a not-for-profit organization that trains teachers in Orton-Gillingham at the initial and advanced level. She holds a BA in social and rehabilitation services from Assumption College as well as an MEd in elementary education, a CAGS in special education, and an EdD in teaching and learning from American International College. Dr. Donah has authored two books: *Improving Phonemic Awareness for Struggling Students of All Ages* (2007) and *Improving Morphemic Awareness Using Latin Roots and Greek Combining Forms* (2008). She may be contacted at sfdonah@comcast.net.

ROBERTA GREEN, EDD

Dr. Roberta Green received a BA in biopsychology from Mount Holyoke College, and she earned an MS in clinical psychology and an EdD in educational psychology from American International College. She has worked at the University of Massachusetts, researching the limbic system of the brain. Recently, she completed a postdoctoral program in school neuropsychology from the Texas Women's College. In twenty years in the field of psychology, Dr. Green has been a school psychologist throughout the Massachusetts region as well as the assistant director of the educational psychology doctoral program at American International College. Currently, she is a full-time practitioner of school psychology and a diplomat of the American Board of School Neuropsychology. She may be contacted at r.green@aic.edu.

ELIZABETH JEAN, MED, ABD

Ms. Elizabeth Jean has served as an elementary school educator and administrator in various rural and urban settings in Massachusetts for more than fifteen years. As a building administrator, she has been instrumental in fostering partnerships with various local businesses and higher education institutions, such as Westfield State University, Springfield College, and Western New England University. Further, she has served as an adjunct professor at Our Lady of the Elms College. In terms of formal education, Ms. Jean received a BS in education from Springfield College and an MEd in education with a concentration in reading from Our Lady of the Elms. She is currently a doctoral candidate in Northeastern University's EdD educational leadership and curriculum development program. She may be contacted at elizabeth-jean23@live.com.

RICHARD D. JUDAH, EDD

Dr. Richard D. Judah has practiced clinical and educational psychology in Massachusetts for over thirty years. He is also a professor of graduate studies and a special education consultant. He has published numerous articles in his field and continues to work with both children and adults with neurologically based learning and behavior disorders. He may be contacted at drjudah@comcast.net.

TONI SPINELLI-NANNEN, EDD

Dr. Toni Spinelli-Nannen received her BA and MS in clinical psychology from American International College, an MEd in school counseling from Westfield State University, and an EdD in educational psychology from American International College. She has attended a Bilingual Institute at the

University of Massachusetts focusing on the education of non–English-speaking children. Most recently, she completed a postdoctoral program in school neuropsychology from the Texas Women's College. In over thirty-five years in the field of psychology and education, she has been a teacher in the federal bilingual program in Springfield, Massachusetts; a school psychologist for Spanish-speaking children; a clinical counselor; an instructor of Spanish for law enforcement and fire department officers; and the director of the school psychology and school counseling programs at American International College. Currently, she is a practicing, nationally certified school psychologist; a diplomat of the American Board of School Neuropsychology; and a professor of education and psychology at American International College. She may be contacted at a.spinelli-nannen@aic.edu.

FRANK E. VARGO, EDD

Dr. Frank E. Vargo is an associate professor in the EdD program at American International College located in Springfield, Massachusetts. He has earned numerous degrees in psychology and education, including an EdD in educational psychology, and has completed formal postgraduate studies and training in clinical psychology and neuropsychology. Dr. Vargo is a licensed psychologist as well as a clinical and developmental neuropsychologist. He holds several school practitioner licenses in areas such as school psychology, school adjustment counseling, guidance counseling, and music teaching. He is also the executive director for the Fireside Center Clinic in Leominster, Massachusetts, and the chief executive officer for the Learning and Teaching International organization. Dr. Vargo has published extensively in the areas of psychology, education, learning disabilities, special education, and counseling. He may be contacted through the following website: www.LTI-FiresideCenter.com.

CPSIA information can be obtained
at www.ICGtesting.com
Printed in the USA
LVHW090203170921
698043LV00014B/94

9 781475 811155